Mountain State Mammals

by Ron Russo
illustrated by Barbara Downs

a guide to mammals of the Rocky Mountain region

Nature Study Guild, Berkeley, California

how to use this book

If you see a mammal, the sighting key on pages 9-11 will help identify it. But outside the large National Parks, most wild mammals are elusive. They'll usually see, hear, or smell you first, avoid showing themselves, and wait quietly for you to move on. So most often the evidence of mammals you find will be one of the following signs:

- footprints, see page 14
- droppings, see page 12
- skulls, jaws, see pages 5-8
- burrows, nests, scratch or chew marks, see pages 17-23

key features

On some illustrations, lines point out traits important to identification.

area covered by this book

This book is about the wild mammals of Idaho, Montana, Wyoming, Utah, Colorado, Arizona, and New Mexico.

dimensions

Unless otherwise indicated, dimensions given here are for length. A single figure (44mm) represents a measurement made on a single specimen. A range (42-50mm) indicates the least and greatest dimensions of a number of specimens.

Track measurements given here are lengths of hind-foot prints left by the animal, and are not the length of its whole hind foot.

Ron Russo is chief naturalist for the East Bay Regional Park District, Oakland, California. Barbara Downs is a freelance illustrator in Berkeley, California.

MAMMAL TRAITS

Mammals differ from other organisms in having fur, large brains, a highly refined sense of hearing, and a variety of skin glands. Mammals also suckle their young and spend an extended time caring for them. Here are some other traits.

Body temperature

Mammals keep warm under a coat of hair or fur. To protect against winter temperatures, many mammals develop thicker, longer fur, which they shed in the spring. Deer get extra insulation from the trapped air inside their hollow hairs. Each species keeps a fairly constant body temperature by panting, sweating, and confining activity to the cooler hours in summer, or to warmer slopes in winter. Body temperature varies, however, among different groups of mammals.

Mammals living in desert regions must confine their activity to the cool of night to avoid overheating and loss of precious body water. Many desert mammals get all the water they need from the food they eat. They control sweating, and concentrate their urine and droppings, retaining as much water as possible. Kangaroo rats have gone a step further in having developed nasal traps which remove moisture from their exhaling breath.

Mammals, in any environment, that are active by night and quiet by day are called **nocturnal**. Sometimes you can spot nocturnal mammals by the reflected shine when their eyes, specially equipped for night vision, are struck by the light of a car or campfire.

Camouflage

The color of mammal hair generally blends with the terrain, which helps mammals to avoid detection by prey or predators. When a predator approaches, many mammals, like hares and rabbits, remain motionless and trust their safety to camouflage and stillness. Most mammals see no color, only shades of black and white. A still, well-concealed animal may never be seen, even at a distance of a meter or so. If the predator gets too close the prey will attempt to flee, a tactic also used by quail and pheasants. In some mammals, like squirrels, all-black (melanistic) individuals are occasionally seen.

Reproduction

Mammals have one of the most successful forms of reproduction in the animal kingdom. The development of the young within an amniotic sac provides nourishment directly from the mother and protection from bacteria. The survival rate of fetuses tends to be high as is the survival of newborns because of extended post-birth care. Although many are born naked and blind, others are ready to go. Antelope fawns are ready to stand and run within a few minutes after birth.

Antlers and horns

Some mammals have antlers or horns growing from their skulls. Male members of the deer family and both sexes of caribou produce antlers. Antlers grow externally from calcium deposited by blood-filled capillaries underneath furred skin. By late summer, growth stops and the furry skin, called **velvet**, is rubbed off against tree trunks and small saplings. (See key, page 20). Antlers are sharpened for use and display during the fall mating season. They are shed in winter, regrown in spring.

In contrast, horns grow from an inner core of calcium-rich blood tissue. Antelope horns are shed annually, but those of bighorn sheep are permanent and grow to spectacular sizes and shapes. Males competing for females judge each others' status by the size and shape of horns, antlers, and physique. In pronghorn antelope and bighorn sheep, the females have smaller horns than males.

Evergrowing teeth

Rabbits and rodents have incisors that grow continuously, an adaptation to grit in their diet which would otherwise wear their teeth to the gumline. Evergrowing teeth are kept under control normally by grit, or by gnawing action. If these animals don't have enough grit in their food, or are unable to gnaw regularly, their incisors will grow outside of their skulls and protrude from their mouths. If unchecked, these teeth will continue to grow until they turn backwards towards the skull, preventing the animal from eating. Starvation and death result.

Territories

Mammals often restrict their activities to a definite area called a **home range**. In order to get enough to eat, attract mates, and survive, mammals often defend all or a part of their home range as their **territory**, and routinely drive off intruders of the same species. A defended territory usually has enough food, shelter, and nesting material to support a male and female of the same species. Non-breeding animals usually exist in unclaimed zones or strips found between two or more territories of their species. Territory owners usually patrol their boundaries, marking them in prescribed locations with scent, urine, or droppings. The size of territories varies from year to year as the availability of food and other essential resources changes. If food is plentiful, territories are smaller than in a lean year. Territories expand in response to scarcity. The territories of non-competing species usually overlap.

Parasites

Wild mammals support a wide variety of hitch-hiking parasites like fleas, ticks, blood-sucking flies, and lice. Parasites can weaken their hosts, and occasionally kill them. Because some of these parasites can transmit diseases like plague and tularemia to people, it is a good idea to **avoid handling dead animals**, especially rodents and rabbits.

Skin glands

Mammals have five different kinds of skin glands. Mammary glands in females produce milk to nurse young. Sweat glands help to cool mammals and get rid of waste products through the pores of the skin. Oil glands lubricate skin and hair. Scent and musk glands produce chemicals to mark territories and communicate.

Careful observation, curiosity, and this guidebook will help you enjoy the mammals of the Rocky Mountain states.

Rocky Mountain Wood Tick
Dermacentor andersoni

These ticks are normal parasites on rabbits, squirrels, chipmunks, and deer, and may bite humans, so while outdoors, check your pantlegs regularly for climbing ticks. At end of day, check the warm parts of your body for ticks. If you find one, DO NOT HANDLE WITH BARE FINGERS. Instead, use tweezers or tissue paper over fingers to grip tick close to head and gently pull it out. You may wish to consult a physician about a tickbite, because ticks in this region carry Rocky Mountain spotted fever, which is transmittable to humans.

Skulls

Dental Formulas

The dental formula for a skull or jaw is made by noting the numbers of each kind of tooth, from the front center to the rear of one side. Separate counts are made for the teeth attached to the skull and those in the jawbone.

A formula of:

$$\frac{1\ 0\ 1\ 3}{1\ 0\ 1\ 3}$$

indicates that one incisor, no canine, one premolar, and three molars should normally be present on each side of both the skull and the jawbone. This formula matches the squirrel teeth illustrated to the right.

Health and age may cause teeth to be missing. So a specimen you find may not precisely match the stated formula.

If you find a skull or jawbone, try to match it with the ones on the next page. The dental formula will appear on the page indicated.

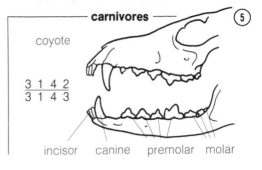

carnivores

coyote

$$\frac{3\ 1\ 4\ 2}{3\ 1\ 4\ 3}$$

incisor   canine   premolar   molar

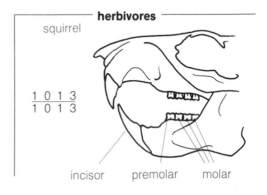

herbivores

squirrel

$$\frac{1\ 0\ 1\ 3}{1\ 0\ 1\ 3}$$

incisor   premolar   molar

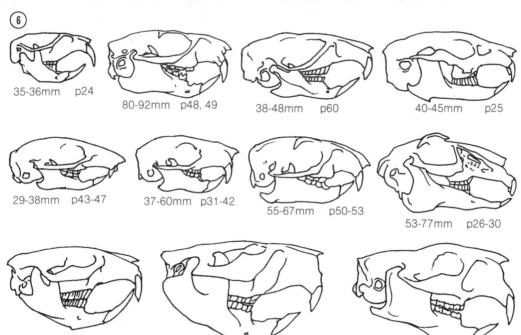

6

35-36mm   p24

80-92mm   p48, 49

38-48mm   p60

40-45mm   p25

29-38mm   p43-47

37-60mm   p31-42

55-67mm   p50-53

53-77mm   p26-30

46-54mm   p56

113-130mm   p54

90-110mm   p58

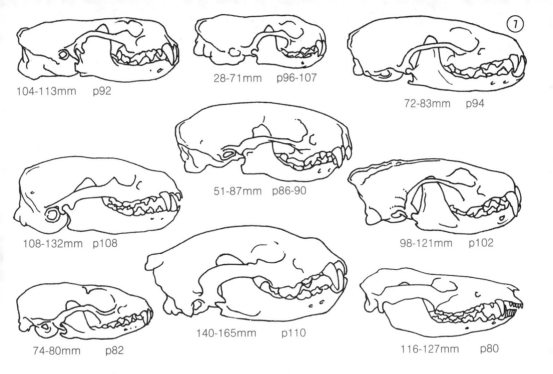

104-113mm   p92

28-71mm   p96-107

①

72-83mm   p94

51-87mm   p86-90

108-132mm   p108

98-121mm   p102

74-80mm   p82

140-165mm   p110

116-127mm   p80

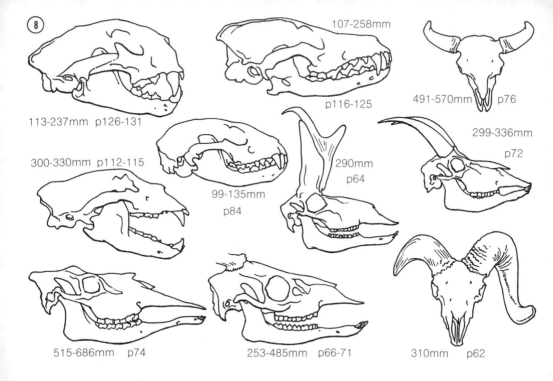

8

107-258mm
p116-125

491-570mm p76

113-237mm p126-131

299-336mm
p72

300-330mm p112-115

99-135mm
p84

290mm
p64

515-686mm p74

253-485mm p66-71

310mm p62

p108

p92

p94

p96-107

p82

p86-90

p102

p84

p110

p112-115

p76

p72

p126-131

p74

p64

p116-125

p66-71

p62

p80

p24

p26-30

p58

p48,49

p25

p60

p54

p50-53

p31-42

p43-47

p56

(12)

3-8mm

chimpmunks p43-47

4-20mm

squirrels p31-42

7-14mm

woodrats p60

25mm

3-5mm

pika p25

20-30mm

porcupine p58

6-18mm

rabbits p26-30

42mm

opossum p80

15-30mm

prairie dogs p50-53

25-40mm

marmots p48,49

55mm

pine marten p94

40-75mm

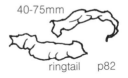
ringtail p82

20-75mm

weasels p96-107

100-150mm

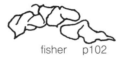
fisher p102

30-50mm

skunks p86-90

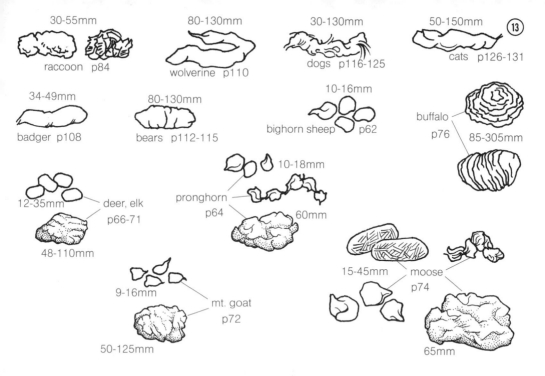

30-55mm
raccoon p84

80-130mm
wolverine p110

30-130mm
dogs p116-125

50-150mm ⑬
cats p126-131

34-49mm
badger p108

80-130mm
bears p112-115

10-16mm
bighorn sheep p62

buffalo p76
85-305mm

12-35mm
deer, elk p66-71
48-110mm

10-18mm
pronghorn p64
60mm

15-45mm
moose p74

9-16mm
mt. goat p72
50-125mm

65mm

(14) Track measurements are for print left by hind foot.

18-24mm p60

18-50mm p31-42

17-27mm p43-47

28-60mm p48,49

15-25mm
p25

32-48mm

p86-90

30-32mm p50-53

53-165mm

p26-30

85mm

p58

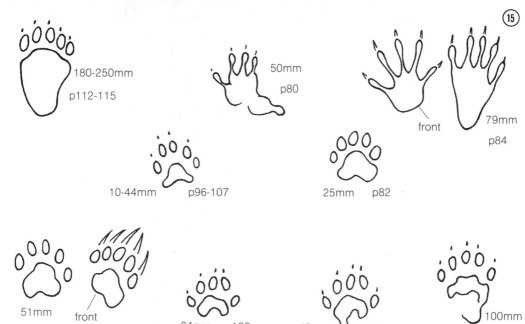

180-250mm
p112-115

50mm
p80

front

79mm
p84

10-44mm   p96-107

25mm   p82

51mm   front

p108

64mm   p102

40mm   p94

100mm

p110

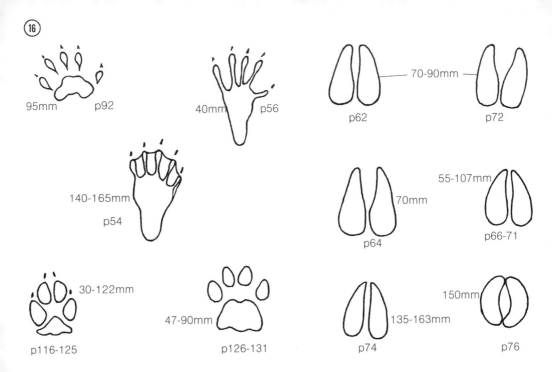

(16)

95mm   p92

40mm   p56

70-90mm

p62   p72

140-165mm

p54

70mm

p64

55-107mm

p66-71

30-122mm

p116-125

47-90mm

p126-131

135-163mm

p74

150mm

p76

If you've found a nest or house of twigs, cut grass or marsh plants, or shredded pine cones and scales, go to page 18.

If you've found a hole leading into a tunnel, go to page 19.

If you've found a linear ridge of smooth soil, often branched, on top of the ground in snow country, spring and summer, see **gophers**, p. 24.

If you've found a round mound of pushed-up soil, no hole, see **gophers**, p. 24.

If you've found a depressed or matted-down area which is:

- made of marsh plants, streamside grasses matted down with tufts of twisted grass, droppings, musky odor, see **river otter**, p. 92.

- less than .5m long, in grassland, sagebrush, or next to rocks or bunchgrass, see **rabbits**, **hares**, p. 26-30.

- over 1m long, in meadow or forest, with or without strong urine scent and droppings, see **deer**, **elk**, p. 66-71.

- about 2m long, in a thicket, matted with leaves, needles, boughs, see **grizzly**, p. 112.

- over 2m long in open grasslands, prairies, or under shade trees, see **buffalo**, p. 76.

- a shallow scraped-out depression on ledges or mountain tops with droppings all over bedding area, see **bighorn sheep**, p. 62.

*A burrow is the front door and hallway, a den is the whole house.

(18) If the nest or house is next to water and is made of:

- matted down marsh plants, 1m high, along stream, pond, or marsh edges, see **muskrat**, p. 56.

- stacked twigs in mounded piles 2-3m high and wide, with mud packed on top, near twig/branch dams, near or in water, see **beaver**, p. 54.

If it's among pine trees or associated with shredded cones, and:

- in high or outer branches of a tree, or at tree base, with chewed pine cones, see **tree squirrels**, p. 32-34.

- at the base of tree, made of shredded pine cones and cone scales, in mounds, 1m or more across, see **red squirrels**, p.33.

If it's a pile of twigs, 1m or so across, at the base of a tree shrub or cactus, in a rock crevice or the back of a cave, see **woodrats**, p. 60, 61.

If it's a stack of cut grass piled under rock ledges or among rockpiles of high mountain areas, see **pika**, p. 25.

If the opening of the hole is:

- less than 6cm across, at the bases of shrubs, trees, fallen logs, with other holes nearby, in mountainous areas, see **chipmunks**, p. 43-47.

- about 5-10cm across, round, in groups of several holes with little or no grass nearby, on slopes or flat ground, see **ground squirrels**, p. 35-39.

- about 10-15cm wide on a large, 1m wide cone-shaped mound, bare ground, in colonies, in plains, grassland, desert habitat, see **prairie dogs**, p. 50-53.

- round, in snow, often with muddy tracks, see **ermine**, p. 100, **mink**, p. 106.

- wider than 20 cm, flat across the bottom, solitary, often with smaller holes nearby, see **badger**, p. 108.

- about 22-38cm wide with mounds or fans of dirt in talus slopes, rock out-croppings, cluttered with medium to large droppings in rock crevices, see **marmots**, p. 48, 49.

- about 50-66cm wide in a grass meadow, bank, rock outcropping with good view of terrain, marked by large dog-like droppings, see **gray wolf**, p. 116.

If you've found:

- a tree with chew marks, gouges, or missing bark, go to **[1]**, next page.

- tree trunks with vertical scratch or claw marks, go to **[2]**, next page.

- tips of tree or shrub branches nipped, pruned, or stripped of leaves, go to **[3]**, p. 22.

- tufts of hair caught on rocks, tree trunks, sagebrush, willows, go to **[4]**, p. 22.

- piles of chewed pine or spruce cones or nuts near logs or at the base of trees in mountainous areas, see **red squirrel**, p. 33.

- a dead animal covered by dirt, snow, leaf and branch litter, or hanging from a tree branch, see **wolverine**, p. 110, **lynx**, p. 128, **mountain lion**, p. 130, **grizzly bear**, p. 112.
  CAUTION: If this is a bear kill, the bear may not be far away. **LEAVE THE AREA IMMEDIATELY**

- signs that don't fit the above categories, go to page 23.

[1] If the chew marks or gouges are:

- deep into one side or around base of a tree, often felling it, near pond or stream, see **beaver**, p. 54.

- higher than a person's head and associated with girdled, bark-stripped areas below, see **bears**, p. 112-115.

- not deeply into the wood with large patches of bark removed, often at several places on the same tree, see **porcupine**, p. 58.

- linear gouges that break through the bark, but not deep into the wood, extending several feet above the ground, see **elk**, p. 70.

- sharp, narrow, vertical, with shredded bark, 1m or so above ground, common on saplings, low branches, see **deer**, **elk**, p. 66-71.

[2] If the bark has vertical claw-puncture marks that are:

- obvious, long, usually associated with extensive damage to the tree, see **bears**, p. 112-115.

- not obvious, in sets which are:

  - under 6cm wide, see **bobcat**, p. 126.

  - over 6cm wide, see **lynx**, **mountain lion**, p. 130.

(22) **[3]** If you've found:

- tips of shrub branches stripped of all leaves, see **deer**, p. 66-69.

- all of the lower branches of a tree or group of trees pruned evenly/horizontally, 2-3m above ground, see **deer**, **elk**, p. 66-71.

- tips of small shrub branches nipped off at an angle under 1m high, see **rabbits**, **hares**, p. 26-30.

[4] If you've found tufts of hair on rocks, tree trunks, sagebrush, or willows near water and the hair is:

- white, in rocky, craggy areas or hanging from trees or shrubs near timberline, see **mountain goat**, p. 72.

- light brown to chocolate brown, usually curly, soft, on large boulders in open areas, prairies, on heavily rubbed tree trunks, or on sagebrush, in parks, see **buffalo**, p. 76, **elk**, p. 70.

- cinnamon to light brown, coarse, usually straight, on tree trunks worn smooth by rubbing, see **grizzly bear**, p. 112.

- chocolate brown to charcoal on shrubs, particularly willow or on ground, near streams, ponds, meadows, see **moose**, p 74.

If you've found other signs like:

- a dam of sticks forming a pond, see **beaver**, p. 54.

- a round, bowl-shaped hole in the ground with wasp or paper nest parts scattered, see **skunks**, p. 86-91.

- large, gaping holes in the ground with claw marks in dirt, overturned rocks, torn up berry bushes, see **grizzly bear**, p. 112.

- extensive patches of ground dug up, rocks overturned, see **hognose skunk**, p. 90. (Could also be feral pigs.)

- long, muddy slides on river banks, see **river otter**, p. 92.

- partially buried droppings with scratches nearby, see **mountain lion**, **bobcat**, **lynx**, p. 126-131.

- tightly bound, twisted, cigar-shaped masses of foil, cellophane, or grass in large, dog-like droppings, see **coyote**, p. 118.

- a tree hole with a gnawed rim, near streams, see **ringtail**, p. 82.

- any other signs, try a larger book. See p. 132.

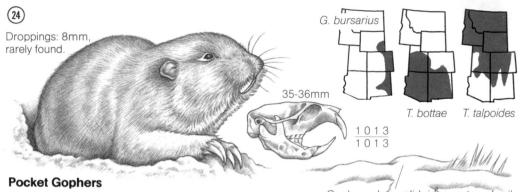

Droppings: 8mm, rarely found.

G. bursarius

35-36mm

$\frac{1\ 0\ 1\ 3}{1\ 0\ 1\ 3}$

T. bottae *T. talpoides*

Pocket Gophers

Geomys bursarius
Thomomys bottae, T. talpoides

Have large, external, fur-lined cheek pouches for carrying food. Squeeze contents out with fore paws; turn pouches inside out for cleaning. Burrowing area may cover 2000 square feet. Gophers' lips close behind upper incisors to keep dirt out of mouths while they dig. Enamel covers fronts of incisors, creating sharp, bevelled edges as backs of teeth wear faster. Gophers are active day, night, year round. Eat roots, tubers, greens. Solitary. Males fight all other gophers on contact, except females in breeding season. Two species rarely live in same field. Sexually mature at three months. Young born mainly in spring, one or two litters per year, two to eleven per litter. Predation low. Enemies: badgers, weasels, snakes, owls, hawks, coyotes, foxes.

Gopher esker: solid ridge on top of soil in snow country, no tunnel underneath.

40-45mm

or

$$\frac{2023}{1023}$$ or $$\frac{2032}{1023}$$

25mm   pellets 3-5mm

15-25mm

Pika, Cony, Rock Rabbit, Piping Hare
Ochotona princeps

Round body, short legs and ears, and dense fur conserve body heat. No visible tail. Common on alpine and fir forest talus slides. Variable color blends with rocks. Territorial. Gives sharp, nasal chirps. Makes "hay piles" of drying vegetation (each one may be a bushel or more). Diurnal. Does not hibernate. Active under snow, using stored hay

for food. Reingests soft droppings for protein, energy, and vitamins. Stores dried marmot droppings for same use. Concentrates urine to conserve water; leaves distinctive white marks on rocks. Young born May-August, naked, blind, three to four per annual litter. Enemies: weasels, martens, coyotes, hawks.

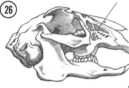

67-75mm

$$\frac{2\ 0\ 3\ 3}{1\ 0\ 2\ 3}$$

18mm

90-165mm

Whitetail Jackrabbit, Whitetail Hare
Lepus townsendii

Gray-brown, often turns white in winter, but always has white tail with slight dorsal stripe. Ears narrower than those of Blacktail. Common in sagebrush and open areas; does not burrow. Can jump five meters on a bound with speeds up to 40 mph. Feeds at night on sage, grass, bark of young trees. Young born furred, eyes open, three to six per annual litter. Enemies include: foxes, coyotes, bobcats, lions, owls, hawks, eagles. Ears of all "Jacks" are long and well-supplied with blood vessels to disperse body heat in hot weather.

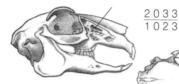

$$\frac{2\ 0\ 3\ 3}{1\ 0\ 2\ 3}$$

66-77mm

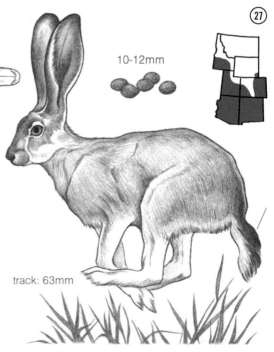

10-12mm

track: 63mm

Blacktail Jackrabbit, Blacktail Hare
Lepus californicus

Gray-brown, tawny. Has large black-tipped ears. Eyeshine is red. Common in sage, cactus, meadow and open grassland country. Places hind feet ahead of front feet in normal gait. Eats green vegetation, shrubs and cacti. Most active early evening and morning. Can run 30-35 mph. Uses a zig-zag running escape pattern. Young are born year round, furry, with eyes open. Enemies include: coyotes, eagles, hawks, barn owls, large snakes.

All rabbits and hares form two kinds of droppings: soft, which are reingested for vitamin and protein nutrition; and hard, which are not.

127mm

53-56mm

$$\frac{2\ 0\ 3\ 3}{1\ 0\ 2\ 3}$$

10-13mm

Snowshoe Hare

Lepus americanus

Changes from dark brown in summer to white in winter. Only tips of hairs turn white. Eyeshine is orange. In swamps, forests, mountain thickets. Home range: about ten acres. Nocturnal. Eats succulent vegetation in summer; twigs, bark, buds, and sometimes frozen carcasses in winter. Does not build nest. Young born April-August, two to three litters per year, two to four per litter. Populations fluctuate dramatically, with peaks every 11 years. Life span in wild about three years.

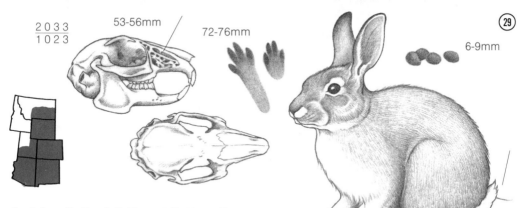

$\dfrac{2\ 0\ 3\ 3}{1\ 0\ 2\ 3}$

53-56mm

72-76mm

6-9mm

Audubon Cottontail, Desert Cottontail
Sylvilagus audubonii

Long ears that are sparsely furred inside distinguish this rabbit from mountain cottontail. In open plains, foothills, low valleys; in grass, sage, pinyon-juniper, deserts. Home range: nine acres for females, up to 15 acres for males. Active in late afternoon, night, and early morning. Stays close to thickets. Eats green vegetation and a variety of fruit, tree bark rarely. Young born naked and blind, in fur nests, throughout the year. May live two years in wild. Vulnerable to marauding domestic dogs. Note: Eastern Cottontail, *S. floridanus,* is found in central, southern Arizona, New Mexico, eastern Colorado, southeastern Wyoming.

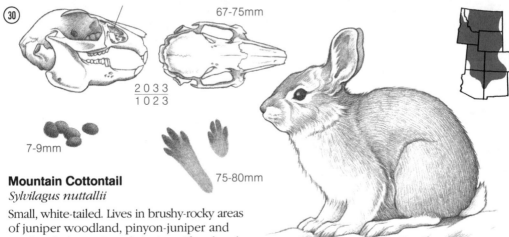

Mountain Cottontail
Sylvilagus nuttallii

Small, white-tailed. Lives in brushy-rocky areas of juniper woodland, pinyon-juniper and sagebrush desert. Long hairs in uniformly colored ears distinguish it from Audubon Cottontail. Nocturnal, but also active in morning. Eats sagebrush, grass and tree shoots. Young born naked, blind, in fur-lined nest in early summer, one to eight per litter. Rabbits in some areas produce several litters per year. Enemies same as other rabbits.

67-75mm

$$\frac{2\ 0\ 3\ 3}{1\ 0\ 2\ 3}$$

7-9mm

75-80mm

CAUTION: All hares and rabbits may carry tularemia or "rabbit disease" which can be transmitted to people. **Avoid handling dead rabbits**, but, if necessary, use rubber gloves.

Squirrel Biology

There are about 11 species of ground and tree squirrels in the Rocky Mountains. Many are active only in late spring and early summer. Some enter summer sleep (estivation) in July when it gets too hot and go directly into fall-winter sleep (hibernation) in October. Most store food for use after awakening from sleep periods. Most species of ground squirrels require habitat where they have an excellent view of the terrain — often where grass is grazed or mowed. Squirrels have fleas which can easily transmit plague to people who handle dead specimens.

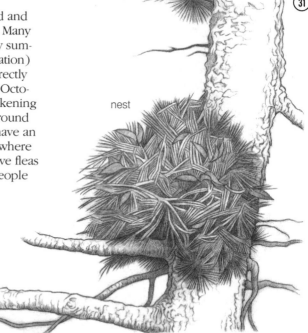

nest

Several species gnaw cones for nuts and sweet sap.

pine cone

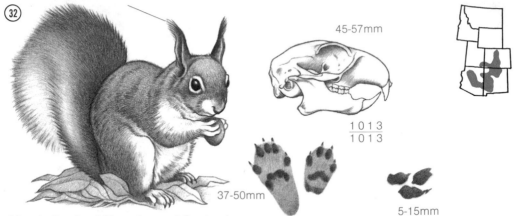

45-57mm

1 0 1 3
———
1 0 1 3

37-50mm

5-15mm

Abert's Squirrel, Tassel-eared Squirrel
Sciurus aberti

Dark, grizzled-gray to black; reddish tint on back. Belly light. Tail all white or white underneath. Found in coniferous forests to 8500 ft, sometimes in pinyon-juniper zone. Active throughout winter, but in extremely cold weather may stay in nest for short periods. Home range: about 20 acres. Eats mostly ponderosa pine seeds, inner bark of pine, mistletoe, truffles, and other plant materials. Stores some seeds at the base of nest tree. Mating chases seen in February-March. Three to four young born in March-April. Enemies: hawks, coyotes, bobcats, autos, hunters.

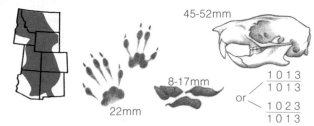

Red Squirrel, Chickaree, Pine Squirrel
Tamiasciurus hudsonicus

Yellowish-reddish, rust-red to gray-red with white-gray belly. Black line along sides in summer. Smallest tree squirrel in its range. Spends more time on the ground than other tree squirrels. Found in conifer, hardwood, and mixed forests. Territorial. Diurnal. Active throughout year. In fall, cuts green cones and buries them in damp soil or creates cone piles at the bases of conifers. In winter, tunnels through snow to get at cone piles. Home range: less than 200 m (220 yd) across. Nests in hollow tree, log, burrow, or tree crotch. Eats mostly pine seeds, but also acorns, berries, eggs, baby birds, fungi. Vigorously protects cone piles. Mates February-March; sometimes again in June-July. Two to seven young born March-April and August-September. Enemies: primarily marten, also coyotes, bobcats, lynx, foxes, weasels, hawks, owls. Lifespan: to ten years.

Note: The introduced eastern fox squirrel, *Sciurus niger,* may occur in Rocky Mountains, most likely in and around city parks, but is limited by the availability of acorns.

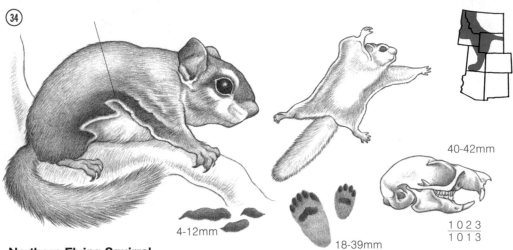

4-12mm

18-39mm

40-42mm

$$\frac{1\ 0\ 2\ 3}{1\ 0\ 1\ 3}$$

Northern Flying Squirrel
Glaucomys sabrinus

Body gray-brown, belly hairs white-tipped, with fur-covered skin membrane between fore and hind limbs used for gliding. In coniferous and mixed forests. Home range: about four acres. The only nocturnal squirrel.

Eats lots of fungi in summer, lichens in winter. Gregarious in winter, may den in groups. Nests in old woodpecker holes or other tree cavities. Young born May-June, two to six per annual litter. Worst enemy: owls.

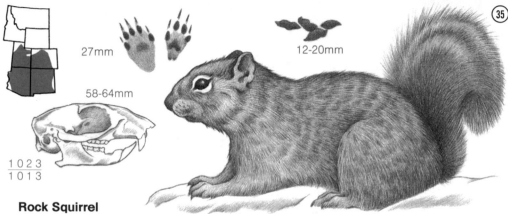

27mm

12-20mm

58-64mm

$\frac{1\ 0\ 2\ 3}{1\ 0\ 1\ 3}$

Rock Squirrel
Spermophilus variegatus

Mottled gray-brown to nearly black mixed with cinnamon-brown over body. Tail buff-brown with white edges. The largest ground squirrel in its range. Found in open rocky areas, oak-juniper woodland, in canyons, and boulder-strewn slopes and flats. Climbs trees. Active early morning, late afternoon. Hibernates for short periods; often out on warm days of winter in the north. Seen sitting on top of rocks. Burrows beneath rocks. Eats juniper berries, mesquite beans, acorns, nuts, cactus, other plants, and carrion. Stores food in den. Mates March-July. Five to seven young born April-August. Two litters per year. Enemies: foxes, coyotes, bobcats, hawks, large snakes. Lifespan: ten years in captivity.

43-48mm   (Tracks illus. p38.)

$\dfrac{1\ 0\ 2\ 3}{1\ 0\ 1\ 3}$

12-20mm

Richardson's Ground Squirrel
Flickertail, Wyoming Ground Squirrel
Spermophilus richardsoni (S. elegans)

Gray, yellowish-gray, cinnamon-buff over back tinged with light brown, faintly mottled. Whitish-buff on lower sides and belly. Found in open prairies, sagebrush, grassland, especially where vegetation is short. Solitary; colonial in favorable places. Issues a shrill whistle followed by a flick of the tail. Hibernates late September to March. May estivate in July to avoid heat. Burrow entrances 9 cm (3.5 in) across with a mound. Eats insects, seeds, leaves, stems. One squirrel stuffed its cheek pouches with 1,302 seeds. Six to eight young born April-May. Enemies: badgers, weasels, snakes, striped skunks, foxes, coyotes, bobcats, owls, hawks, eagles. Vulnerable to sylvatic plague. Only 12% of young males survive to start their second season, because they disperse before females and are more subject to predation. Lifespan: three to four years.

(Tracks illus. p38.)

49-57mm

10-16mm

$\dfrac{1\ 0\ 2\ 3}{1\ 0\ 1\ 3}$

Columbian Ground Squirrel
Spermophilus columbianus

Bushy-tailed, rusty ground squirrel. Dark, rusty-reddish feet, legs, face, and belly. Mottled-gray underparts. Sometimes grayish with black mixed in over back with indistinct buff spotting. Found in meadows, edges of open forests, cultivated fields, alpine fields, arid grasslands. Diurnal. Colonial. Starts estivation in July, slips directly into hiberna-tion. Sleeps seven to eight months a year. Seals off sleeping chamber with dirt plug. Emerges February-March. Eats green vegetation, seeds, grass, stems, bulbs, tubers, and insects. Stores food in sleep chamber prior to estivation. Two to seven young born late March-April. Enemies: hawks, eagles, coyotes, foxes, bobcats, badgers, snakes.

Best hind track measurements are for this species. Other ground squirrels may vary slightly.

10-20mm

27mm

Uinta Ground Squirrel
Spermophilus armatus

$\frac{1\ 0\ 2\ 3}{1\ 0\ 1\ 3}$ 45-48mm

Head, face, ears cinnamon with splash of gray on top of head. Middle of back brownish, sides pale. Tail buff mixed with black. Found in meadows, edges of fields with green vegetation, dry sage, sage-grass mix, and campgrounds, up to 8,000 feet. Colonial. Emerges from hibernation March-April. Starts estivation in July, then goes directly into hibernation. Eats green vegetation, seeds, insects, carrion. Four to six young born April-May. One litter per year. Badger is primary predator.

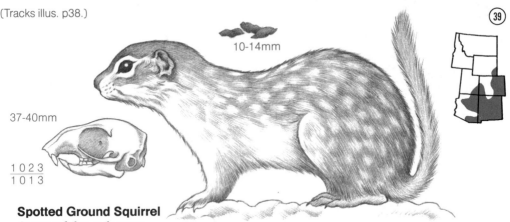

10-14mm

37-40mm

1 0 2 3
1 0 1 3

Spotted Ground Squirrel
Spermophilus spilosoma

Small gray-brown or red-brown squirrel with indistinct squarish white or buff spots on back. Tail thin, not bushy. Found in open forests, scattered brush, parks, sandy soil areas. Diurnal. Active throughout the year, but some may hibernate. Shy, secretive. Stays low to the ground. Territorial behavior limited to area near burrow entrances. Burrows are beneath bushes, rocks, with entrance about 50 mm (2 in) wide. Home range: about 3.5 acres. Spotted ground squirrel eats green vegetation, seeds, insects. Five to seven young born in spring. One litter per year in north, but two litters per year in south. Enemies: hawks, owls, foxes, coyotes, weasels, large snakes.

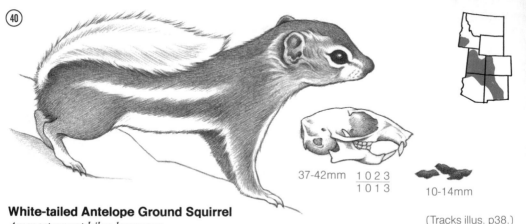

37-42mm $\dfrac{1\ 0\ 2\ 3}{1\ 0\ 1\ 3}$

10-14mm

White-tailed Antelope Ground Squirrel
Ammospermophilus leucurus

(Tracks illus. p38.)

Buff in summer, gray in winter with white belly and distinctive white stripe on sides. Edges of tail have black-tipped hairs; white underneath. Found in deserts, foothills, gravelly soils, among scattered junipers. Burrows have pathways radiating away, no mound at entrance. This ground squirrel uses burrows of other animals. Active throughout the year in southern range, hibernates in northern range. Solitary. Runs with tail held up or over back. Usually on ground but climbs yuccas, cacti to feed. Eats seeds, fruit, insects, meat. Stores food. Five to fourteen young born in early spring. A second litter may occur in some areas. Enemies: foxes, coyotes, badgers, hawks, large snakes.

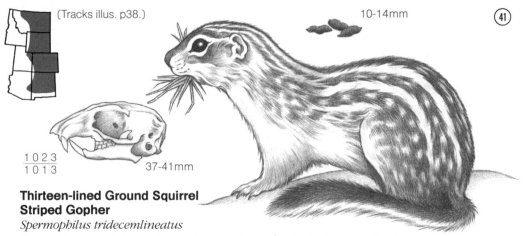

(Tracks illus. p38.)

10-14mm

41

$$\frac{1\ 0\ 2\ 3}{1\ 0\ 1\ 3}$$

37-41mm

Thirteen-lined Ground Squirrel
Striped Gopher
Spermophilus tridecemlineatus

Brownish, with 13 alternating dark and light longitudinal lines (white lines sometimes broken into spots). Belly whitish. Found in short grass prairies, roadsides, cemeteries, parks and wherever grass is grazed or mowed. Diurnal; especially active on warm days. Solitary; sometimes colonial in hibernation. Enters den in October and plugs entrance with dirt. Emerges in March-April. Eats caterpillars, grasshoppers, grass, weed seeds, carrion. Mates in April. Seven to ten young born in May. In southern range, a second litter may occur in late summer. Enemies: hawks, badgers, weasels, coyotes, snakes, feral cats, autos.

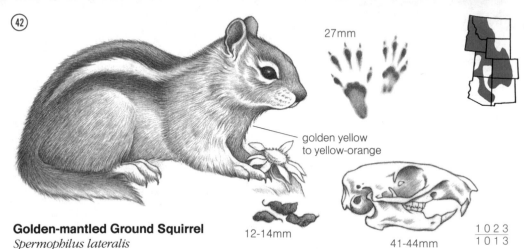

27mm

golden yellow
to yellow-orange

12-14mm

41-44mm

$$\frac{1\ 0\ 2\ 3}{1\ 0\ 1\ 3}$$

Golden-mantled Ground Squirrel
Spermophilus lateralis

Chipmunk-like. Back gray-brown, belly white, head and shoulders golden yellow, sides white with two black borders. In moist conifer forests to above timberline. Home range: less than 200 yards, with two to five animals per acre. Burrows to 30 m (100 ft) long, branched, with round openings near logs, stumps, tree roots or boulders. Young born early summer, two to eight per annual litter. Prepares for hibernation by adding layer of fat in fall. Cleans self by rolling in dust, then combing fur with teeth and claws. Enemies: hawks, weasels, coyotes, bobcats, lynx, foxes, owls.

Chipmunks

About five chipmunk species occur in the Rocky Mountains. Some are distinguishable only by bone characteristics, geography, habitat. Chipmunks in the more humid, forested areas tend to be more heavily pigmented than those from arid regions. All have internal cheek pouches for food gathering. All are diurnal.

Instead of storing body fat like true hibernators, chipmunks store large quantities of food in their burrows for use during winter and early spring. At higher elevations, the first snows in late October or early November send chipmunks below ground where they remain until spring. They wake periodically to feed on the stored seed. At lower elevations, chipmunks are inactive for short periods and emerge from burrows during warm weather.

The bulk of chipmunk diet is seed, mostly from plants of the sunflower family. One researcher found a cache with 35,000 seeds from 20 different plant species. Chipmunks also eat berries, insects, and occasionally carrion. Their enemies are hawks, weasels, bobcats, lynx, coyotes, foxes and snakes.

Gestation takes about one month. Young born in spring, two to seven per litter, usually one litter per year. Young are able to breed the following spring. Life span is about five years.

(Skull, tracks, droppings illus. p46.)

Yellow Pine Chipmunk
Tamias amoenus

Colors bright tawny to pink-cinnamon, with black and white back and side stripes; ears black in front, white in back. In open conifer forests, and rocky areas with brush or pines. One cache of food contained 67,970 items with 15 different kinds of seeds, corn, and a piece of bumblebee.

Least Chipmunk
Tamias minimus

Color varies from yellowish-gray with tawny dark stripes to rich gray-tawny with black stripes. Sides often orange-brown. Lightest colored of all chipmunks. In low sagebrush deserts to high mountain conifer forests. Nests beneath stumps, logs, rocks, in ground. Lines burrow and nest with moss, lichens, grass, and feathers. Runs with tail up.

Cliff Chipmunk
Tamias dorsalis

(Skull, tracks, droppings illus. p46.)

Gray with indistinct dark stripes middle of back and sides. Lower sides and feet yellowish. Bushy tail rusty-red underneath. Indistinctly striped gray fur serves as protective coloration against rocks. Found in pinyon-juniper forests, lower edges of pine forests. Known for sharp bark followed by tail twitch at the rate of about 160 per minute.

29-38mm

typical chipmunk skull

$$\frac{1\ 0\ 2\ 3}{1\ 0\ 1\ 3}$$

17-27mm

3-8mm

Colorado Chipmunk
Tamias quadrivittatus

Head, sides, rear gray. Sides with tawny-rust tones, dark-brown stripes. Colors bright. Ears blackish in front, white behind. Tail black-tipped. Found in coniferous forests, rocky slopes, and ridgelands.

Sizes of skulls, tracks and droppings of all chipmunks are within above ranges.

Uinta Chipmunk
Tamias umbrinus

(Skull, tracks, droppings illus. p46.)

Similar to Colorado Chipmunk. Gray over back and head with broad, dark-brown side stripes. Tawny-buff on sides. Tail white-edged, black-tipped. Found in coniferous forests, mixed woods, junipers, scrub oaks to timberline, 11,000 ft. Often seen in trees. Eats seeds, fruit, berries.

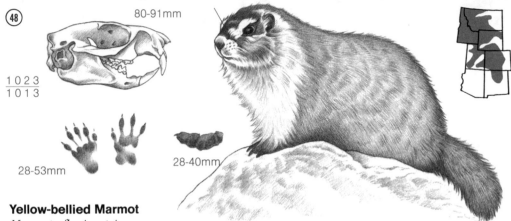

Yellow-bellied Marmot
Marmota flaviventris

Heavy-bodied rodent common on talus slopes and roadside rock piles in high mountains. Shares habitat with pikas. Body yellow-brown to rusty-brown. All-black individuals occur. Burrow is in talus pile; entrance to 23 cm (9 in) wide, with fan of packed dirt. Uses large boulder nearby as lookout. Chirps or whistles when alarmed. Often in colonies with a dominant male who may have harem of several females. Eats green vegetation. Diurnal. Develops layer of fat for hibernation October-March. One litter of three to six blind, naked young born in April. Lifespan to about ten years. Enemies: eagles, coyotes, bobcats, lynx, lions.

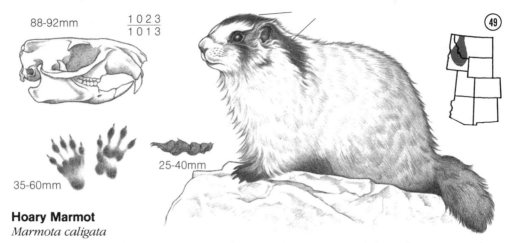

88-92mm

$$\frac{1\ 0\ 2\ 3}{1\ 0\ 1\ 3}$$

25-40mm

35-60mm

Hoary Marmot
Marmota caligata

Large. Silver-gray back and sides; brownish rump, white belly. Black and white markings on head, shoulders. Tail large, bushy, red-brown. Feet dark-brown to black. Silvery fur is good camouflage among rocks. Found on mountain talus slopes near timberline, in alpine meadows. Diurnal. Diet is almost entirely grass, some other green plants.

Makes burrows with large fans or mounds 22-38 cm (8.7-15 in) wide. Often wrestles playfully with others. Has loud, high, shrill alarm whistle. Hibernates October through February. Mates soon after emerging from den. Four to five young born late spring or early summer. Enemies: bears, coyotes, foxes, bobcat, lynx.

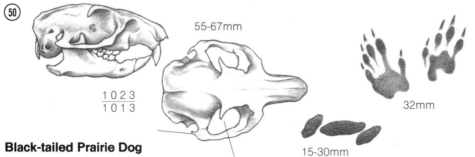

55-67mm

$\dfrac{1\ 0\ 2\ 3}{1\ 0\ 1\ 3}$

32mm

15-30mm

Black-tailed Prairie Dog
Cynomys ludovicianus

Chunky, ground dwelling squirrel. Sandy-tan, lighter underneath and around eyes. Front feet have long claws for digging. Black-tailed prairie dog is extremely vocal, with rapid series of yaps, trills, whistles, and chattering sounds. Also communicates by touch. Found in open grasslands, prairies, and mesas. Diurnal. Usually seen sitting upright on top of burrow mound. Sleeps in burrow to avoid heat of midday. Uses special chambers in burrow for feces; when these fill, new chambers are dug. Eats grass and forbs, occa-sional insects. Mates March-April. Four to six young born April-May. Colonial; large colonies are divided into small neighborhoods or territories. "Dog towns" can hold several thousand individuals. One "town" in Texas was estimated to hold over 400 million "dogs." Enemies: coyotes, badgers, eagles, hawks, bobcats, snakes. Black-footed ferrets, now extinct in the wild, were once their primary predator. Lifespan: Seven to eight years.

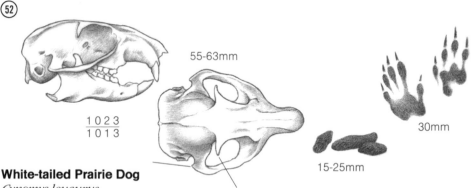

55-63mm

$$\frac{1\ 0\ 2\ 3}{1\ 0\ 1\ 3}$$

30mm

15-25mm

White-tailed Prairie Dog
Cynomys leucurus

Stout-bodied ground squirrel. Sandy-brown over back. Light underparts. Yellowish nose. Found in high country to 12,000 ft; open, slightly brushy country; scattered junipers, pines; sagebrush and high plains. Less colonial and social than black-tailed prairie dog. Builds burrow mounds up to 1 m high, 2.4 m wide (3 by 8 ft), which are sometimes used by burrowing owls and rattlers. Adult shows little fear of rattlers. Eats grasses, forbs, and seeds. Estivates in July. Enters den for winter sleep in October; during this period, may awaken and feed on underground roots, tubers. Emerges and mates March-April. Two to ten young born in early May. Enemies: bobcats, coyotes, badgers, hawks, eagles. Bubonic plague once devastated prairie dogs in Colorado. Floods and fire kill some. Lifespan: four to five years.

113-130mm

top view of molar

$$\frac{1\ 0\ 1\ 3}{1\ 0\ 1\ 3}$$

Droppings: 35-40mm, rarely found.

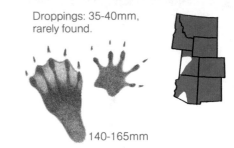

140-165mm

Beaver
Castor canadensis

Large, dark brown rodent with scaly tail. Skull has chestnut brown incisors. Beaver lives in mountain streams, ponds, lakes. Its transparent eyelids cover eyes during dives to allow continuous vision while underwater. When alarmed, it slaps water with tail to warn other beavers. Gnaws trees until they fall: uses them for food; for building materials for bow-shaped dams; for domelike lodges; and for scent mounds, which mark territory and attract mates. Burrows up through snow to gnaw trees at surface; as snow level changes, several gnawed bands may be left, creating a "totem pole" effect. Active through-out year. Feeds mostly on aspen, cotton-wood, willow, and birch. Also eats cattails, tules, willow roots, pond lilies. Droppings of coarse, sawdustlike material are rarely found because they decompose rapidly. Probably mates for life. Kits born furred, eyes open, four per litter. Stay with parents for two years. Lifespan 10-12 years. Young killed by otters. Adults occasionally killed by coyotes, foxes, bobcats, and lions. Almost trapped out of existence in nineteenth century to supply soft, fine fur for hats, robes, and coats, but now reestablished over most of its former range.

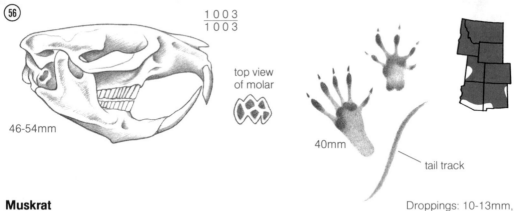

56

$$\frac{1\ 0\ 0\ 3}{1\ 0\ 0\ 3}$$

top view
of molar

46-54mm

40mm

tail track

Droppings: 10-13mm,
rarely found.

Muskrat

Ondatra zibethica

Aquatic rodent with dark brown, glossy fur, and tail flattened vertically for swimming. Muskrat is excellent swimmer, stays submerged for 15 minutes. Mouth closes behind protruding incisors, making underwater chewing possible. Muskrat builds house of matted vegetation to 1.2 m (4 ft) high; burrows in banks; makes feeding platforms. Marks territory with mats of cut plants and scent. Active day and night. Eats aquatic plants, clams, crayfish, frogs, fish. Breeds April-August, has up to five litters per year of four to seven naked, blind young. Babies swim at one week. Live five to six years. Enemies: raccoons, otters, mink, and people.

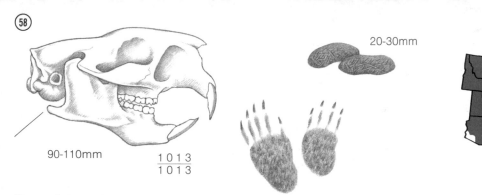

90-110mm

$$\frac{1\ 0\ 1\ 3}{1\ 0\ 1\ 3}$$

20-30mm

85mm

Porcupine
Erethizon dorsatum

Gray-brown, chunky body, high arching back, short legs. Has about 30,000 hair quills on back, rump, and tail. When alarmed, flips tail, releasing quills from skin. Quills are not thrown. Once in an enemy's flesh, the quills work deeper, can be fatal. Porcupine has no other defense. In forests and some open areas. Active year around. Mostly nocturnal, but suns in trees. Solitary in summer, lives colonially in winter. Eats green plants and cambium layer under bark of trees. Fond of salt. Mates in fall. One baby born May or June, headfirst, with soft quills aimed backward. Fishers circle porcupines, biting at face until able to inflict mortal wound. Mountain lions, coyotes, bobcats also attack porcupines.

36-40mm $\frac{1\ 0\ 0\ 3}{1\ 0\ 0\ 3}$

7-14mm

molar top view

18mm

Woodrats

Presence of gray-tawny woodrats is indicated by bulky nests of twigs at bases of trees, shrubs, cactus, or in rock crevices, old buildings. Also, by large accumulations of droppings in rock crevices. "Packrats" earn their name by stashing anything they fancy in nests. Nocturnal. Territorial. Respond to disturbance by drumming or thumping with hind feet or tails. Woodrat tails have hairs, unlike "old world" rats. Woodrats feed on green plants, nuts, berries, fungi, seeds. Most species give birth to one to four young per annual litter. Enemies include owls, foxes, coyotes, bobcats, and large snakes.

White-throated Woodrat
Neotoma albigula

Throat hair white to base. Found in brushland, rocky cliffs with small caves. Builds house amid cactus, in brush or small caves. Eats cactus, mesquite beans, seeds. Home range: about 100 feet. Population usually 10-20 per acre.

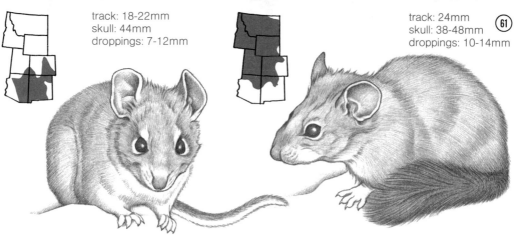

track: 18-22mm
skull: 44mm
droppings: 7-12mm

track: 24mm
skull: 38-48mm
droppings: 10-14mm

Mexican Woodrat
Neotoma mexicana

Found among rocks and mountain cliffs. Eats acorns, nuts, seeds, fruit and fungi. House not a conical pile like that of other woodrats, but a loose collection of sticks and debris jammed into crevices, or under cliff ledges, under logs, tree roots, deserted buildings.

Bushy-tailed Woodrat
Neotoma cinerea

Most widespread woodrat. Squirrel-like, bushy tail distinctive. Found along rimrock, rock-slides, pine forests of high mountains. House made of sticks, bones, other material in rock crevices, under logs. Eats green vegetation, twigs, shoots. May store food as dry hay.

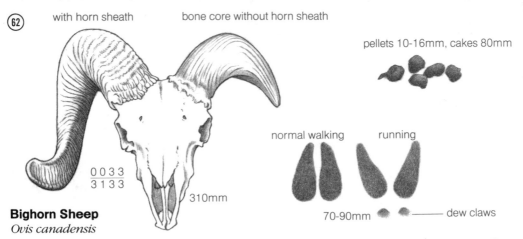

with horn sheath

bone core without horn sheath

pellets 10-16mm, cakes 80mm

normal walking   running

0 0 3 3
3 1 3 3

310mm

70-90mm ● ● —— dew claws

Bighorn Sheep
Ovis canadensis

Gray-brown to ash gray; belly, rump white. Horns in rams thick, coiled; in ewes, not coiled, small. Sexes separate in summer, together in fall. Rams of equal size challenge each other for ewes, rear and charge at 20 mph to butt heads loudly. Skull double thick with struts of bone to cushion impact. Bighorn eats sedge, grass, sagebrush, alpine plants. Bed a depression smelling of urine with droppings all over, used for years. Single lamb born May-June, stays with herd. Lives 14 years. Golden eagles take lambs. Threatened by weather, disease, loss of viable habitat, human intrusion. Several isolated races or populations occur.

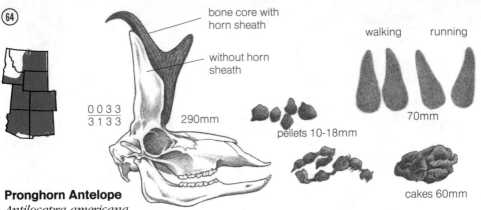

bone core with horn sheath

without horn sheath

walking running

$\frac{0\ 0\ 3\ 3}{3\ 1\ 3\ 3}$

290mm

70mm

pellets 10-18mm

cakes 60mm

Pronghorn Antelope
Antilocapra americana

Upper body tan; chest, belly, rump white. Short, erect mane. Antelope raises rump hairs to flash warning when alarmed. Sheds outer covering of horns after breeding season, permanent core remains. Can run at 44 mph, with short bursts to 70 mph. Fastest animal in western hemisphere. Can leap horizontally four to eight meters, but can't jump fences. In open prairies, sagebrush plains.

Forms summer bands up to 12 animals; winter bands to 100. Eats grasses, cacti, sagebrush (*Artemisia*), rabbitbrush (*Chrysothamnus*). Droppings are in segmented, stringy masses when antelope eats succulent grass; small pebble-like forms when it browses. Antelope breeds in fall. Young born April-June, unspotted, odorless. Twins common. Lifespan ten years. Chief enemy: coyotes.

Rocky Mountain Mule Deer

Odocoileus hemionus hemionus
Color varies: yellow-brown to reddish in summer, sooty gray in winter. Tail mostly white with small black tip. White rump patch. This is the largest North American mule deer with some bucks reaching 470 lbs. Mule deer is found in open woods or forest. Active at dusk and dawn, but may be seen at other times. Usually beds down at mid day. Follows habitual daily activity patterns, visiting same area night after night. It is forced down to lower elevations for fall and winter when snow accumulates at high altitudes. Eats shrubs, trees, forbs, grasses, sedges, and rushes. Bucks solitary, but may be in bands before and after rut in September-October. Mating follows rut. First-birth does have single fawns in June; second-birth and older does usually have twins. Mothers quickly lick odorless newborns dry and coax them to walk to get away from the birth fluids, which attract predators. Mule deer gain weight in summer, early fall. Lose 20-22% of their weight in late fall and winter. Enemies: lions, coyotes, golden eagles, grizzlies, feral dogs. Habitat and food limitations are key factors in deer loss. Females usually live 10-12 years (22 maximum); males about eight years (16 maximum).

Antlers in old bucks are multi-branched. Size and number of branches is influenced by age, health of deer, quality of food. First set of four points (two on each side) may occur at age two. Extraordinary antlers with 20 points on each side have been recorded. Antlers drop December-March. New antlers, covered in velvet, begin to grow in April-May. Initial growth is slow, but increases rapidly in summer, often exceeding one cm (0.4 in) per day. Velvet drops off in August when bucks scrape antlers against saplings, often stripping bark away.

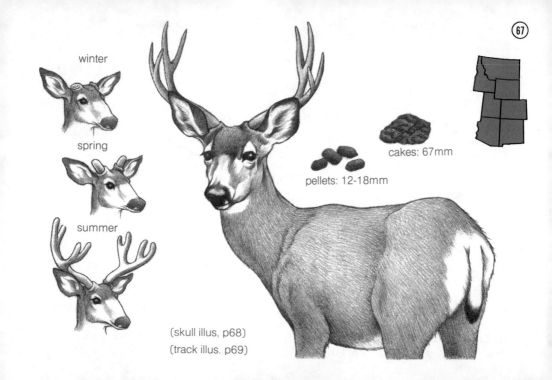

winter

spring

summer

67

pellets: 12-18mm

cakes: 67mm

(skull illus, p68)
(track illus. p69)

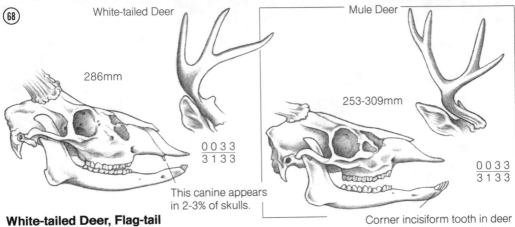

White-tailed Deer

286mm

$\frac{0\ 0\ 3\ 3}{3\ 1\ 3\ 3}$

This canine appears in 2-3% of skulls.

Mule Deer

253-309mm

$\frac{0\ 0\ 3\ 3}{3\ 1\ 3\ 3}$

Corner incisiform tooth in deer & elk is technically a canine.

White-tailed Deer, Flag-tail
Odocoileus virginianus

Coat reddish in summer, blue-gray in winter. Raises all-white tail when running. In forests, brushlands, swampy meadowlands. Home range: about one mile. Runs to 40 mph. Jumps 9 m (30 ft) horizontally, 2.4 m (7.9 ft) high. Bucks rub antlers on tree trunks and saplings close to ground to mark territory, remove velvet, and to sharpen them. Breed November-February. Does often have twins after first breeding cycle. White-tailed deer stamps feet and snorts when nervous. Lives 16 years in wild. Rips vegetation away, rather than nipping as rabbits do. Same enemies as other deer.

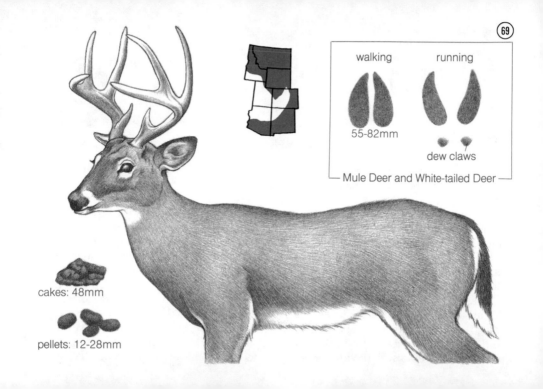

walking

running

55-82mm

dew claws

Mule Deer and White-tailed Deer

cakes: 48mm

pellets: 12-28mm

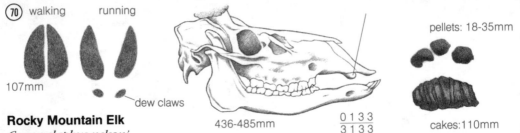

walking   running

107mm

dew claws

pellets: 18-35mm

Rocky Mountain Elk
Cervus elaphus nelsoni

436-485mm

$\frac{0\ 1\ 3\ 3}{3\ 1\ 3\ 3}$

cakes: 110mm

Head, neck, legs are dark brown, while sides and back are gray-brown in winter, reddish-brown in summer. Yellowish-tawny rump. Males average 700 lbs. Winter-summer migrations involve moving 30-40 miles. In winter, 1,000 or more can be on range in the Jackson Hole Elk Refuge, but severe winters can bring over 15,000 animals to this range. In summer, small groups of elk usually herd together. Elk beds down on open hillsides in storms or sometimes in heavy timber to avoid severe storms. Seeks snowbanks and north slope forest cover on hot days. Bulls shedding velvet with bloody antlers seek high, open points where stiff breezes keep the flies off. Summer diet is 30-80% grass and forbs. Browse from shrubs, trees comprises over half of the diet at other times. In September, the piercing bugling sounds of bulls ring through the high country as they declare their interest in mating and begin forming harems. One calf, rarely two, born by June. Mountain lions, bears, wolves, and coyotes take young and weak adults. Large numbers die due to lack of winter forage, disease, and predation. Elk were once slaughtered just for their upper canine "bugler" teeth, which were used for watch charms.

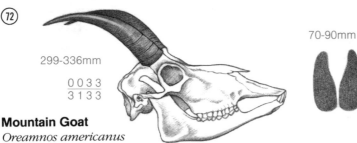

299-336mm

$$\frac{0\ 0\ 3\ 3}{3\ 1\ 3\ 3}$$

70-90mm

pellets 9-16mm,

cakes 50-125mm

Mountain Goat
Oreamnos americanus

Compact, stocky body with yellow-white to white shaggy fur, long in winter, shorter in summer. Eyes, nose, hooves, horns black. Hooves have sharp outer rims and rubbery soles that grip and provide traction on steep, smooth surfaces. Occasionally loses footing and falls to death. Both sexes have slightly backward-pointing, dagger-like horns; horns and skull are fragile. Not a true goat. Found in rocky, mountainous, craggy terrain above timberline. Winter home range: often as small as 200 acres. Prefers lowest possible south-facing cliffs as well as high ridges where wind removes snow. Active morning, evening, and occasionally on moonlit nights. Usually in groups of two to four in summer, in larger groups on bedding grounds in winter storms. Eats grasses, sedges, other green plants in summer; shrubs in winter; mosses and lichens year round. Breeding battles rarely occur. Mates November-December. One kid, sometimes twins or triplets, born May-June. During first winter 27-72% of kids die, more in severe winters. Golden eagles knock kids off ledges. Mountain lions, bob-cats, grizzly bears, coyotes take a few goats. Greatest killers are avalanches, rock slides. Lifespan: 12 years in wild.

515-686mm

pellets 15-45mm, cakes 65mm

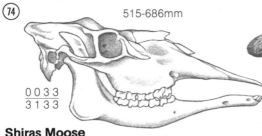

willow

sagebrush

diet

dry food

wet food

Shiras Moose

Alces alces shirasi

Dark brown with gray legs, overhanging snout. Palm-like antlers spread to 206 cm (81 in). Largest "deer" in North America, with males to 1,400 lbs. Found in or near water, in spruce, aspen forests with lakes, swamps, in willow thickets, sometimes in sage flats. Most active at night, but seen anytime. Solitary, except for cow-calf pairs, but may herd in winter. Antlers, shed in December-February, are quickly gnawed for calcium by rodents. Moose may submerge almost completely or roll in mud to avoid mosquitos, black flies. Can run 35 mph. Eats mostly aquatic vegetation during summer. Browses on twigs, buds, bark, especially willow in winter-spring. Known to walk on front knees to reach low-growing plants on sage flats. Breeds September-October. Bulls usually avoid battle with each other, but occasionally lock antlers and starve to death. Usually one, but sometimes two reddish-brown calves born May-June. **Caution:** While normally shy and retiring, moose are unpredictable and dangerous. Cows fiercely protect calves and rutting bulls will charge. Enemies: grizzly bears, wolves. Lifespan: to 20 years.

walking

running

dew claws

135-163mm

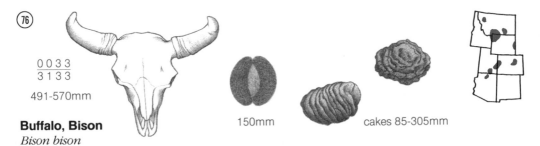

$$\frac{0\ 0\ 3\ 3}{3\ 1\ 3\ 3}$$

491-570mm

150mm

cakes 85-305mm

Buffalo, Bison
Bison bison

Dark brown with massive head, high shoulder hump, long shaggy hair on shoulders, front legs. Largest terrestrial animal in North America, 800-2,000 lbs. Both sexes have horns. Can gallop to 32 mph. Diurnal; most active in early morning, late afternoon, moonlit nights. In woods horn and head rubs leave a ring of missing bark on trees. In open areas, large boulders are often rubbed. Buffalo are grazers, but occasionally browse, eat berries, lichens, horsetails. Buffalo have a "pecking-order" system of dominance. Bulls form temporary pairs and breed several cows sequentially, July-September. One to two yellowish-red calves born by May. Caution: **Buffalo are extremely dangerous at all times, especially during the breeding-calving season.** Lifespan: normally 15-20 years, but some live 30 years. Once found in open plains, prairies and open woods from Ohio to Wyoming, Saskatchewan to Texas. In 1600 there were about 70 million. The entire culture of plains Indian tribes centered on the buffalo. Mass extermination began around 1830, encouraged by the government, as an attempt to subdue Indians. By 1900 about 1,000 buffalo remained. Today, over 30,000 thrive mostly in parks.

Bats

Many species in this area. Only true flying mammals. Furry bodies, naked wings. Hearing is acute. Use echolocation to avoid objects and locate food, emitting 30-60 squeaks per second from nose or mouth. Muscles control ears so that bats hear only returning sound waves when flying. Bats capture insects in flight or on ground, consuming tons of destructive pests. Drink from streams, ponds, lakes, in flight; often captured by large trout, bass. Feed around city street lights; hang head down on porch walls and eat large insects, leaving droppings on walls. Metabolism lowered when asleep to conserve energy. Some bats are solitary, others colonial. Some migrate, others hibernate. One or two young born late spring. Some bats carry rabies, so **handling them is dangerous**.

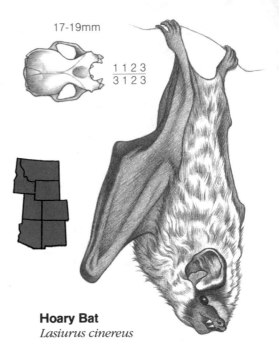

17-19mm

$\frac{1\ 1\ 2\ 3}{3\ 1\ 2\ 3}$

Hoary Bat
Lasiurus cinereus

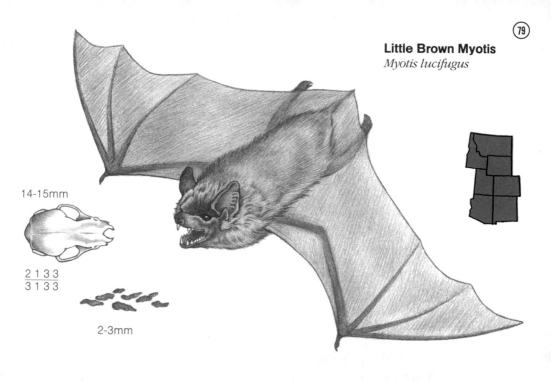

Little Brown Myotis
Myotis lucifugus

14-15mm

$\frac{2\ 1\ 3\ 3}{3\ 1\ 3\ 3}$

2-3mm

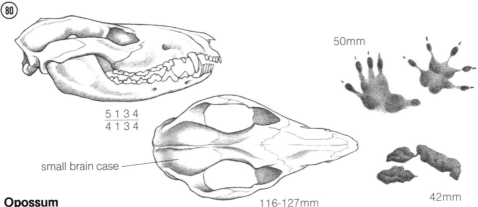

$$\frac{5\ 1\ 3\ 4}{4\ 1\ 3\ 4}$$

small brain case

50mm

116-127mm

42mm

Opossum

Didelphis marsupialis

Only pouched mammal in U.S. Scruffy, gray body with prehensile tail. Thin, black, hairless ears and part of tail may be missing due to freezing. Opossum feigns death when threatened. Thrives in urban, rural, and woodland areas. Nests in hollow trees, logs, culverts, brush piles, under houses. Eats fruit, vegetables, nuts, insects, carrion, eggs. Noc-turnal. Solitary. Does not hibernate; stays in den for several weeks in cold weather. Has one to two litters, January to October. One to 14 embryos crawl out of womb to pouch covering 13 teats. Embryos could all fit in teaspoon. Nurse for two months. Five to seven normally survive to juvenile stage. Lifespan about seven years. Many killed by autos.

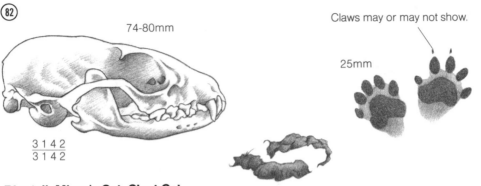

74-80mm

Claws may or may not show.

25mm

3 1 4 2
3 1 4 2

40-75mm

Ringtail, Miner's Cat, Civet Cat

Bassariscus astutus

Yellowish-gray above, whitish-buff below. Body cat-like with fox-like face. Claws partially retractile. Found in brushland, near water, rocky places in canyons, talus slopes, boulder piles. Dens in cliffs between or under large rocks, in hollow trees, stumps, logs, or abandoned buildings. Nocturnal. Often hunts in pairs. Populations usually less than five to ten per square mile. Home range: up to a square mile. Ringtail is an excellent climber. Can release a foul-smelling fluid when threatened or fighting. Eats insects, mice, rats, squirrels, rabbits, carrion, birds, snakes, frogs, toads, and fruit. Mates in early April in southern part of range. Two to four young born May-June. Enemies: bobcats, great horned owls, people. Lifespan: 14 years in captivity.

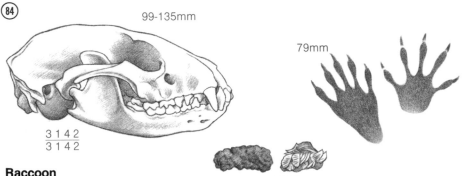

99-135mm

79mm

$$\frac{3\ 1\ 4\ 2}{3\ 1\ 4\ 2}$$

30-55mm

Raccoon
Procyon lotor

Color salt-and-pepper. Playful, curious, good swimmer. Feeds mostly along streams, lakes, ponds, but will wander from water. Dens in hollow trees, logs, rock crevices, or ground burrows. In cold weather, may sleep for several days; does not hibernate. Chiefly nocturnal, but occasionally about in day. Especially active in autumn. Solitary. Diet varied: fruits, nuts, grains, insects, frogs, fish, crayfish, birds' eggs. Washes food to enhance sense of touch in toes, which helps it discern non-edible matter. Leaves droppings at base of den tree, on large branches, rocks, logs across streams. Mates in February or March. Two to seven young born April or May. In fall, young raccoons may disperse up to 160 miles, but mostly less than 30 miles. Chief enemies: dogs, hunters, autos. Raccoon can defend self well against a single dog. Not abundant in northern Rockies.

85

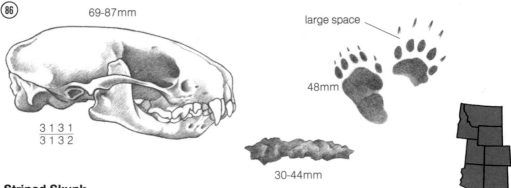

69-87mm

large space

48mm

30-44mm

$$\frac{3\ 1\ 3\ 1}{3\ 1\ 3\ 2}$$

86

Striped Skunk
Mephitis mephitis

Bold coloring warns predators. When threatened may snarl, stamp feet, raise hind legs, click teeth, arch tail, turn toward enemy. This failing, shoots jet spray of musk to 4.5 m (15 ft) as final defense. Adult skunk needs about ten acres. Digs own burrow, uses one abandoned by other animal, or may use protected space under house (unless repelled by mothballs). Nocturnal. Does not hibernate; may be inactive for weeks in winter. Male solitary; female may den with others in winter. Eats variety of vegetable matter, insects, grubs, mice, eggs, frogs, and also yellowjackets and their nests, leaving large holes in ground. Four to seven young born in May, follow mother single-file until June or July. Chief carrier of rabies. Enemies: great horned owls, golden eagles.

$$\frac{3\ 1\ 3\ 1}{3\ 1\ 3\ 2}$$ 51-62mm

32mm

30-40mm

Spotted Skunk

Spilogale gracilis

Boldly marked, with pom-pom-like tail. More active than other skunks. Stands on front feet with back and tail arched over head as defense warning. Climbs trees to escape enemies. One spotted skunk may hunt over 160 acres. Less territorial than other skunks, more socially tolerant, thus 13 or more spotted skunks may be found in a square mile.

Nests in burrows beneath buildings, rock piles. Several may den together in winter. Eats mice, birds, eggs, insects, carrion, and some vegetable matter. Mates in September. Two to seven young born May-June. Owls, cars are worst enemies; foxes and bobcats take a few.

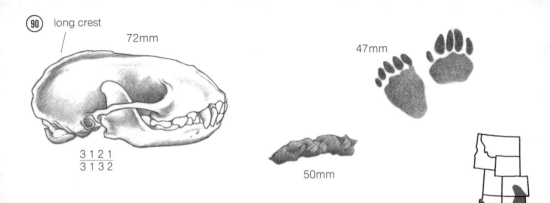

long crest

72mm

$$\frac{3\ 1\ 2\ 1}{3\ 1\ 3\ 2}$$

47mm

50mm

Hog-nosed Skunk, Rooter Skunk

Conepatus mesoleucus

Large white area starts at top of head and covers back, tail. Uses long, naked, pig-like snout for rooting up insects. Found in partly wooded, brushy, and rocky areas. Primarily nocturnal, but about in the day. Solitary. Dens in crevices of cliffs. Eats insects mostly, also small rodents, reptiles, roots. Evidence suggests this skunk may be immune to rattlesnake venom. Mates in March. Two to four young born April-May. Enemies: people, autos. Little is known about natural predators of this skunk, although great horned owls and coyotes are likely suspects.

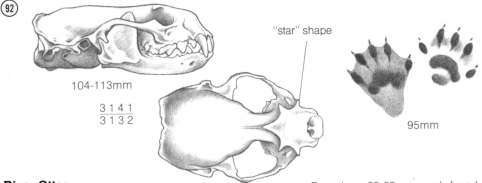

104-113mm

$$\frac{3\ 1\ 4\ 1}{3\ 1\ 3\ 2}$$

"star" shape

95mm

River Otter

Lutra canadensis

Droppings: 60-65mm, rarely found.

Rich brown above, silvery below. Can stay underwater two to three minutes because pulse slows and skin flaps close ears and nostrils. Lives in large rivers, streams, sloughs, or in beaver ponds. Home range: to nine miles inland, variable distance along shore. Travels at night. Enlarges and uses burrows of other animals, such as beaver and muskrat, for dens along water's edge. Makes river bank slides 30 cm (1 ft) wide. Snow slides show track marks. When on land, river otter spends most of its time frolicking, chasing its tail, or playing tag. Rolls in cattails or grass to dry off and to mark territory with musk, droppings. Females breed just after giving birth, in March to May, to one to four blind, helpless, furry pups, which must be taught to swim.

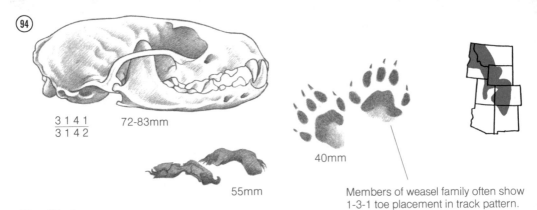

$$\frac{3\ 1\ 4\ 1}{3\ 1\ 4\ 2}$$ 72-83mm

55mm

40mm

Members of weasel family often show
1-3-1 toe placement in track pattern.

Pine Marten

Martes americana

Brown body with orange-yellow throat and chest. Lives in deep coniferous forests, large high-mountain rock piles. Dens in hollow trees. Active night, early morning, late afternoon and cloudy days. Spends lots of time in trees. May travel 15 miles in search of food. Eats tree squirrels, mice, voles, pikas, hares, some berries. Buries surplus meat.

Breeds in midsummer; fertilization of eggs by sperm is delayed, embryos form in early winter. Young born in April, one to five in litter. May breed after first year. Males use scent glands under belly skin to mark territory, attract mates. Martens are curious. One male was live-trapped 77 times in a row. Enemies: fishers, large owls.

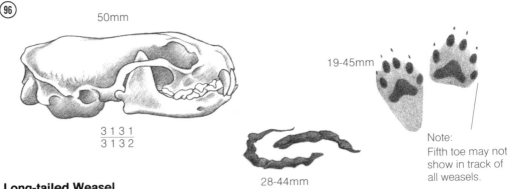

50mm

$$\frac{3\ 1\ 3\ 1}{3\ 1\ 3\ 2}$$

19-45mm

Note:
Fifth toe may not
show in track of
all weasels.

28-44mm

Long-tailed Weasel
Mustela frenata

Body brown, with black face and tail tip, underparts beige-yellow, except in snow country, northern areas, where shorter fall days stimulate color change to all white with black nose, eyes, and tail tip. Habitat varied: forest, brush, farmland, near water. Chiefly nocturnal, but active day and night throughout year. Eats mostly mice — often caches several dead mice under log. Also eats rabbits, squirrels, chipmunks, birds, etc. Ounce for ounce, the most ferocious, efficient mammal predator. Leaves droppings on logs, rocks, stumps. Lines nest, in abandoned den of other animal, with fur of mice and "trophies" (bones, feathers) of hunts. Three to nine nearly naked, blind young are born in May. Enemies: hawks, owls, cats, coyotes, foxes, minks, martens, fishers.

97

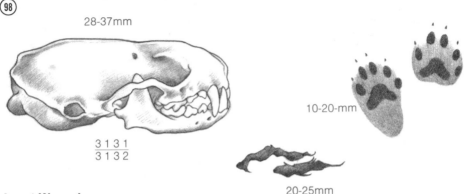

28-37mm

$$\frac{3\ 1\ 3\ 1}{3\ 1\ 3\ 2}$$

10-20-mm

20-25mm

Least Weasel
Mustela nivalis

Brown above, whitish below in summer. Feet white. White all over in winter, except in southern range. Lacks black-tipped tail of ermine. Smallest carnivore in North America. Found in meadows, fields, brushy areas, and open woods. Uncommon. Home range: about two acres when food is plentiful; 25-65 acres when scarce. Most active at night.

Dens in shallow burrow made by mouse, gopher, mole or other animal that it has killed. Burrow entrance about 2.5 cm (1 in). Eats mostly mice, voles, but takes insects, moles. Enemies: large owls, minks, other weasels, hawks, foxes, martens. Lifespan: about three years, but to ten years in captivity.

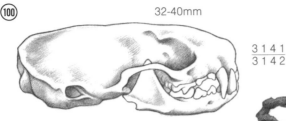

32-40mm

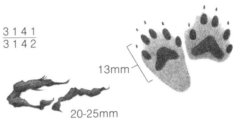

$$\frac{3\ 1\ 4\ 1}{3\ 1\ 4\ 2}$$

13mm

20-25mm

Ermine, Short-tailed Weasel
Mustela erminea

Dark brown above, white below in summer. Tail brown with black tip. In northern range, all white in winter except black tail tip, eyes, and nose. Molts twice yearly in April-May and October-November. Found in open woodland, brushy areas, grasslands, wetlands, farmlands, forests, talus slopes. Dens have several entrances under logs, rock piles, tree stumps. Ermine is inquisitive, territorial, nocturnal, occasionally about in day. Home range: 30-40 acres. Populations of 20 per square mile in good years. Hunts mainly on ground; will pursue prey into water, under snow pack, up trees. Eats mostly mice, also shrews, young rabbits, birds. One study found that a female brought 78 mice, 27 gophers, 34 chipmunks, three woodrats, and four ground squirrels to her den over 37 days. Mates by July. Development of fertilized embryos delayed. Four to nine young born April-May. Enemies are great horned owls, martens, eagles, but ermine die more often from severe winters with little food. In winter, long-tailed weasel is also called ermine because of white coat.

winter

summer

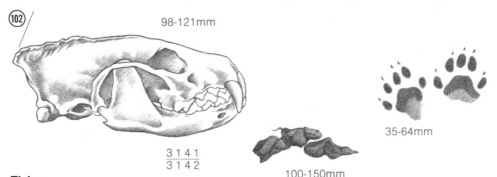

98-121mm

$$\frac{3\ 1\ 4\ 1}{3\ 1\ 4\ 2}$$

35-64mm

100-150mm

Fisher

Martes pennanti

Dark brown to near black with white-tipped hairs over most of the body (frosted look). Grayish head. Claws white. Found in forests, logged areas. Active day and night. Solitary. Dens in hollow tree, in ground, rock crevices. Male's home range: about ten square miles. Doesn't catch fish ("fisher" is misnomer). Eats snowshoe hares, marmots, squirrels, woodrats, birds, carrion, fruit, ferns. One of the few predators of porcupines. Contrary to myth, which claims porcupines are flipped to expose vulnerable belly, fishers attack porcupines head-on, inflicting major wounds. Scat often contains porcupine quills. Fishers mate soon after females give birth to one to four young March-April. Development of embryos delayed. Enemies: mountain lions. Some die from porcupine quills. Lifespan: about ten years.

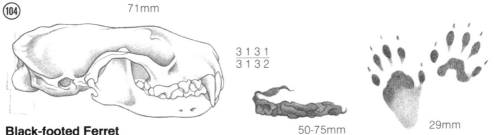

71mm

$$\frac{3\ 1\ 3\ 1}{3\ 1\ 3\ 2}$$

50-75mm

29mm

Black-footed Ferret
Mustela nigripes

Back buff, yellowish to whitish. Black-tipped hairs scattered over body. Nocturnal, solitary, secretive. When prairie dogs are scarce, it eats mice, gophers, ground squirrels, birds, eggs, small snakes. Mates in March-April. Development of the fertilized embryo is only slightly delayed. One to five young born May-June. Enemies: eagles, large owls, and coyotes. Formerly found only in association with black-tailed prairie dogs, its principle food. Black-footed ferret is now believed to be extinct in the wild. Massive campaigns to exterminate prairie dogs, loss of range, and susceptibility to viral distemper caused the ferret's disappearance from the wild. As of early 1989, there were a total of 58 ferrets alive in zoos and captive breeding programs. Successful husbandry and the development of a vaccine for distemper has saved this ferret from total extinction. If their numbers continue to expand and suitable prairie dog colonies are located where both will be protected, ferrets may be reintroduced into the wild after 1991. If you find this ferret, **do not disturb it**. Report discovery to authorities.

former range

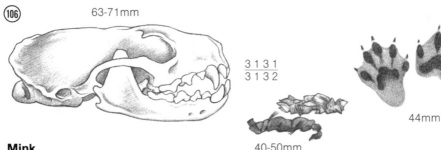

63-71mm

$$\frac{3\ 1\ 3\ 1}{3\ 1\ 3\ 2}$$

40-50mm

44mm

Mink

Mustela vison

Sleek body with lustrous fur. Rich, dark brown with a white chin patch and sometimes small white spots on chin, throat. Found along streams, lakes, ponds, marshes. Chiefly nocturnal. Solitary. Excellent swimmer. Uses temporary dens along stream or lake banks; sometimes muskrat den, beaver lodge, or hollow log. Home range: to 1100 acres. Territorial. Uses discharge as strong as a skunk's to mark boundaries. Deposits scat on beaver lodges, rocks, logs near den. Eats muskrats, rodents, birds, frogs, crayfish, and fish; one mink den contained 13 freshly killed muskrats, two mallards, and one coot. Mates January-March. Two to six young born April-May. Breeds at one year. Enemies: foxes, bobcats, great horned owls, lynx, coyotes. A full grown muskrat in deep water can drown a mink. Adult mink kill more of their own species than all other predators combined. Also killed by tularemia and rabies. Mink may chew off its own foot to escape from steel trap.

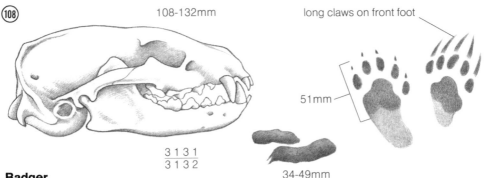

108-132mm

long claws on front foot

51mm

$$\frac{3\ 1\ 3\ 1}{3\ 1\ 3\ 2}$$

34-49mm

Badger
Taxidea taxus

Coat yellow-grizzled gray. Badger has poor eyesight, strong senses of smell and hearing. Loose skin allows twisting, turning in tight spaces to catch food, defend self. In arid grassland, plains, deserts. Badger digs to catch food, escape, rest, den, and to bury droppings and extra food. Its burrow entrance is 20 to 30 cm (8-12 in) wide, elliptical, with flat bottom. It eats rabbits, gophers, squirrels, mice, rattlesnakes, yellowjackets. Coyotes may follow badgers to steal the prey they flush from burrows. Badger is solitary, active day or night. May sleep for weeks during cold weather. Changes dens almost daily in summer. One to five cubs born blind, furred, February to May. Enemies are bears and lions, who do not find badgers easy prey because their squat forms, sharp teeth, strong neck muscles are major defensive advantages. Many badgers are killed by autos.

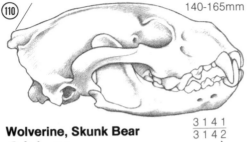

140-165mm

Wolverine, Skunk Bear
$\frac{3\ 1\ 4\ 1}{3\ 1\ 4\ 2}$

Gulo luscus

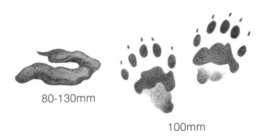

80-130mm

100mm

Dark brown to blackish, pale around the head, with two broad yellowish-beige stripes that start at the shoulders and join at the rump. Has poor eyesight, but swims, climbs well, has good sense of smell. Solitary and elusive. Active day or night. In remote wilderness areas near timberline. Range in lower 48 states shrinking due to human intrusion and low reproduction rate. At 35-60 lbs, the largest member of the weasel family. Incredibly fearless; known to drive bears and mountain lions off their kills. Often trails wolf packs to feed on remains of their kill. Known to clean trap lines of captured animals. Eats carrion, larvae, eggs, beaver, deer, porcupine, squirrels, and birds. Marks food caches with foul-smelling musk that repels other carnivores. Covers caches with dirt or snow, or leaves prey hanging over tree branch. Dens in any sheltered place. Home range: about 1,000 square miles for a male, shared with two to three females. Mates April-August with embryonic development delayed until January. Two to three young born February-April every two to three years. People are its only enemy.

310-330mm

$$\frac{3\ 1\ 4\ 2}{3\ 1\ 4\ 3}$$

250mm

130mm (60mm diam.)

Grizzly Bear
Ursus arctos

Yellowish-brown to black with white-tipped hairs. Claws of front feet to 10 cm (3.9 in) long. Largest North American land carnivore: to 1,700 lbs; most are 800-1,200 lbs. Found in semi-open country, mountainous terrain. Primarily nocturnal, but about in day during fish runs. Generally solitary with little tolerance for each other. Usually well spaced along fishing stream. Vicious fights break out occasionally. Males kill and eat females. Grizzly gains as much as 400 lbs to sustain it through winter sleep. Dens in cave, crevice, hollow tree or protected place. Eats fish, carrion, large mammals, mice, squirrels, marmots, insects, pine nuts, berries, fungi. In some areas it feeds heavily on a variety of plant material. Caches remains of large animals under piles of branches, leaf litter, soil. **Caution: Move away from such a find as quickly as possible, since bear is likely nearby.** Although it generally avoids contact with people, grizzly bear may attack without apparent provocation in close quarters. Can run up to 30 mph. Home range: usually less than 25 square miles. Mates in late spring. Development of embryos delayed until early fall. Young, usually twins, born January-March, every other year. Low nutrition and cub killing by males are major causes of annual loss. Hunters have eliminated this bear from 13 western states. Its existence in the lower 48 states is precarious. Lifespan: 15-34 years.

300mm

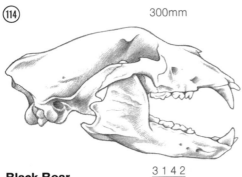

80-110mm
(30-50mm diam)

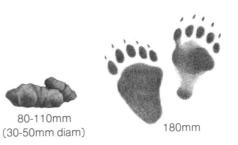

180mm

Black Bear
Ursus americanus

$$\frac{3\ 1\ 4\ 2}{3\ 1\ 4\ 3}$$

Body black or cinnamon. Has keen sense of smell, climbs trees easily. Can run 30 mph in short bursts. Can range 15 miles. Dens under downed trees, in hollow logs or trees, other shelter. Solitary, except in garbage dumps. Mainly vegetarian, but also eats fish, small mammals, eggs, carrion, honeycomb, bees, garbage. Does not hibernate. In fall, bears add thick layer of fat to sustain them during winter sleep; bears without enough fat are active during winter. Mates June to July, every other year. Two to three cubs born in winter den. Lifespan 30 years. "Bear trees" have tooth marks as high as bear stands, claw marks above, to mark territory. Bears are dangerous when surprised, hungry, feeding, injured, or with cubs. Use of claws, pancreas as mythical aphrodisiacs is causing decline of bears outside parks.

claw marks

⑮

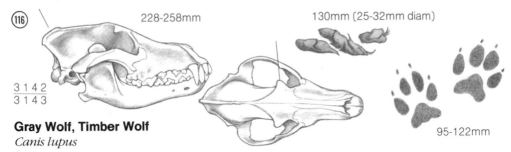

228-258mm

130mm (25-32mm diam)

$\dfrac{3\ 1\ 4\ 2}{3\ 1\ 4\ 3}$

95-122mm

Gray Wolf, Timber Wolf
Canis lupus

Color varies greatly (white to black), but usually grizzled gray. Males to 175 lbs. Found in northern tundra, forests. Rare in lower 48 states. Territory may cover 100 to 260 square miles. Wolf is highly social, normally living in family pack of four to seven animals. Uses howling to keep the pack together. Maintains a strong dominance hierarchy. Uses scent posts marked with urine. Hunts mainly at night, but about in day. Den entrance is large, marked by fan or mound of dirt, scraps of prey. Wolf eats mostly large animals like caribou, moose; also many rodents, birds, fish, berries, and insects. Can run for 30 mph for short distances in pursuit of prey. Mates February-March. Stays with mate for life. About seven pups (usually) born April-June. All members of pack care for young. Enemies are mostly people who persecute wolves, although grizzly bears discovering den may kill pups, and some wolves are injured or killed when hunting large prey or fighting among themselves. Wolves are critical to the health of large herbivores, because they cull out sick, injured, and genetically inferior animals. Lifespan: 10-18 years.

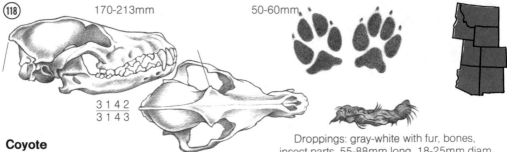

170-213mm   50-60mm

3 1 4 2
3 1 4 3

Coyote
Canis latrans

Droppings: gray-white with fur, bones, insect parts, 55-88mm long, 18-25mm diam.

Color and size variable. Mountain coyotes are larger, have longer fur than desert coyotes. Coyote is vocal at night with a series of yaps, a long howl, then short yaps. Holds tail between legs when running. Can reach 40 mph. Leaves dog-like track. Population, range increasing despite hunting, poisoning campaigns. Widespread. Dens along river banks, well-drained sides of canyons, gulches. May enlarge badger or squirrel burrows. Chiefly nocturnal but active any time. Often hunts in pairs. Omnivorous, but mostly eats small rodents, rabbits, squirrels. Droppings gray, with some seeds, but mostly fur, bones, insect parts, reptile skin, feathers; occasionally solid foil, plastic, or grass, which helps remove tapeworms. Mates January-February. Six to seven pups born April to May, raised by both parents. Livestock losses blamed on coyotes often the work of dogs. Coyotes kill many grass-eating rodents, earning protection from some ranchers.

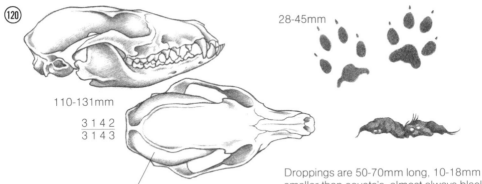

28-45mm

110-131mm

$$\frac{3\ 1\ 4\ 2}{3\ 1\ 4\ 3}$$

Droppings are 50-70mm long, 10-18mm diam., smaller than coyote's, almost always black with stringy ends, berry seeds, fur, etc.

Gray Fox
Urocyon cinereoargenteus

Salt-and-pepper gray with rusty neck, legs, feet. Less vocal than other foxes. Can run, in short bursts, 28 mph. Only fox which climbs trees to escape or to hunt. Mainly in woodland, brushland. Dens in hollow trees, logs, under rock ledges, or in culverts; may have several escape dens nearby. Den area often marked by accumulation of droppings, bones. Gray fox is nocturnal, but often seen in day. Eats small rodents, insects, birds, eggs, fruit, acorns; in some areas, diet is largely cottontail rabbits, ground squirrels, berries. Two to seven pups are born March-April, dark brown, eyes closed. Hunt on their own at four months. Afflicted with many diseases, parasitic worms. Enemies: domestic dogs, bobcats, lions, people. Poison bait intended for coyotes kills many gray foxes.

dark mane

reddish rusty

(121)

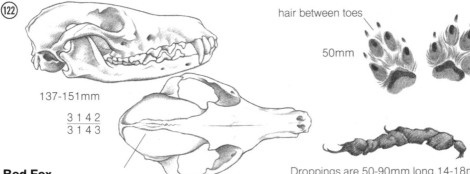

hair between toes

50mm

137-151mm

$\dfrac{3\ 1\ 4\ 2}{3\ 1\ 4\ 3}$

Droppings are 50-90mm long, 14-18mm diam. May resemble those of gray fox.

Red Fox

Vulpes vulpes

Rusty-red, but several color phases exist. White-tipped tail a key feature. In cultivated land, wooded areas, brushland, high mountains. Range is expanding. Mostly nocturnal, also active early morning, evening. Eats fruit, insects, crayfish in summer; birds, mice, rabbits, squirrels in winter. Solitary. Den usually in open area, or along stream, in rock pile. May use enlarged den of badger or marmot. Entrance 30 cm (1 ft) wide, with fan of packed dirt, bones, droppings; one to three smaller, less conspicuous escape holes nearby. Red fox establishes den after mating in January-February, abandons it by late August when family disperses. Four to eight pups born March-May. After several weeks, parents deliver live prey so pups can practice killing. Young males disperse up to 150 miles from birthplace. Enemies: bobcats, coyotes, golden eagles, people.

white

nearly black legs, feet

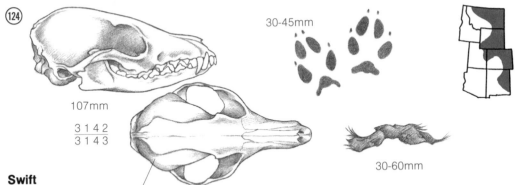

(124)

30-45mm

107mm

$$\frac{3\ 1\ 4\ 2}{3\ 1\ 4\ 3}$$

30-60mm

Swift

Vulpes velox

Buff-yellow above, whitish below. Tail has black tip. Dark spots under eyes. Found in shortgrass prairies and other arid areas. Solitary. Can run to 25 mph. Nocturnal. Nightly hunting circuit may be 16 miles long. Home range: about seven square miles for males. May use old badger or marmot den; den has three or four entrances, each 22 cm (8.7 in) wide, on mound of earth with scattered bones and scraps of prey. Swift mates for life. Breeds January-February. Three to five young born March-April; stay with family until August. Swift eats mostly rabbits, ground squirrels, rats, mice, insects. Also grasses and berries. Sometimes catches prey under snow. Enemies: mostly people. Once nearly exterminated from most of range due to trapping and habitat loss; now recovering and returning to some portions of former range. The swift is closely related to the kit fox.

wolf coyote red fox gray fox swift

Compare sizes.

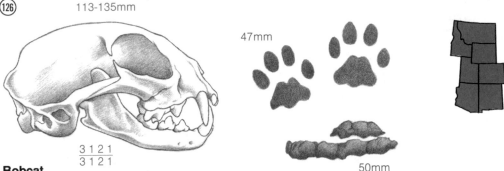

113-135mm

47mm

$$\frac{3\ 1\ 2\ 1}{3\ 1\ 2\ 1}$$

50mm

Bobcat
Felis rufus

Gray-brown to reddish. Ear tufts used like antennae to aid hearing. Good climber. Gets name from "bobbed" tail. In almost every habitat, life zone. Home range: up to 75 square miles. Mostly nocturnal, also seen in daytime. Solitary. Often rests on branches, atop large rocks to watch for passing prey. Eats rabbits, mice, squirrels, porcupines, woodrats, cave bats, small, weak deer. Caches large kills. Droppings are like dog's or coyote's, but often partially buried, with scratch marks on ground. One to seven (average two to three) kittens born April-May in den of dry leaves in hollow log, under rock ledge or fallen tree. Southern animals may have two litters per year. Lifespan 25 years. Marks territory by urinating on rocks or tree trunks, making scent posts. Uses tree trunk as scratching post. Often killed by poison bait intended for coyotes.

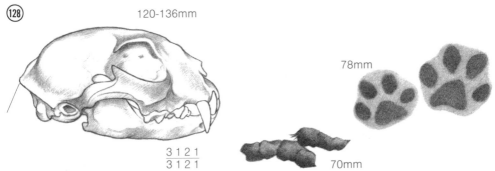

120-136mm

78mm

$$\frac{3\ 1\ 2\ 1}{3\ 1\ 2\ 1}$$

70mm

Lynx, Canada Lynx
Felis lynx

Light gray with yellowish wash over back. Underparts gray, buff-tawny with indistinct black spots. Summer fur shorter, reddish. Ear tufts enhance hearing. Large, thickly furred feet allow silent stalking and good footing in soft snow. Primarily nocturnal. Solitary. Found in northern forests, swamps, remote areas. Creates scent posts by urinating on trees, stumps. Dens in hollow logs, beneath roots, other sheltered places. Home range: to 90 square miles. Populations peak every nine to ten years coinciding with prey cycles. Lynx frequently rests in trees, waiting to pounce on passing prey. Eats snowshoe hares primarily; also takes rodents, birds, occasionally carrion. Partially buries large prey with snow, litter. Mates in late winter. Two kittens (usually) born May-July. Enemies: wolves, mountain lions, people. Lifespan: 15-18 years (in captivity).

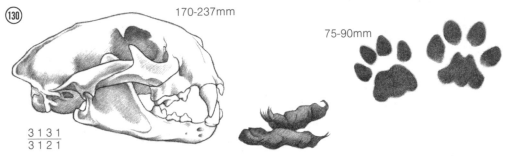

170-237mm

75-90mm

$$\frac{3\ 1\ 3\ 1}{3\ 1\ 2\ 1}$$

76-150mm

Drawn from pellet droppings
in desert. All cat droppings
are partially buried.

Mountain Lion, Cougar, Puma
Felis concolor

Yellowish, grayish, tawny. Habitat generally
wilderness, but may hunt in rural areas.
Male may travel 25 miles in one night.
Strongly territorial. Mostly nocturnal. Rarely
seen. Has voice like tomcat's, greatly magnified. Uses tree trunks as scratching posts.
Solitary. Eats large mammals; one deer per
week forms half of diet. Has more success
catching old, weak, less alert deer, thus keeps
herd healthy. Also eats coyotes, porcupines,
beavers, rabbits, marmots, raccoons, birds,
sometimes livestock. Covers remains of
large kill with branches, leaves. Often partially
buries droppings. Adults breed every two
to three years. One to six furry, spotted kittens born midsummer, raised by female for
one to two years. Enemies: people. Lions are
important predators that should be protected from indiscriminate hunting.

Bibliography

Allen, Thomas B. eds. *Wild Animals of North America,* National Geographic Society, 1979.

Armstrong, David M. *Rocky Mountain Mammals,* Rocky Mountain Nature Association, 1975.

Burt, William H. and Richard P. Grossenheider, *A Field Guide to the Mammals,* Houghton Mifflin, 1974.

Chapman, Joseph A., George A. Feldhammer, eds. *Wild Mammals of North America,* Johns Hopkins University Press, 1982.

Clark, Tim W. and Mark R. Stromberg, *Mammals of Wyoming,* University of Kansas, Museum of Natural History, 1987.

Crump, Donald J., eds, *Book of Mammals, Vols. I, II,* National Geographic Society, 1981.

De La Fuente, Felix R., *Wanderers of Desert and Prairie,* Orbis Publishing Co., 1970.

Haley, Delphine. *Sleek and Savage: North America's Weasel Family,* Pacific Search Press, 1975.

Halfpenny, James. *A Field Guide to Mammal Tracking in Western America,* Johnson Books, 1986.

Jones, J. Knox Jr., David M. Armstrong, Robert S. Hoffman, Clyde Jones. *Mammals of the Northern Plains,* University of Nebraska Press, 1983.

Murie, Olaus. *A Field Guide to Animal Tracks,* Houghton Mifflin, 1974.

Nowak, Ronald M., John L. Paradiso, *Walker's Mammals of the World, Vols. I, II,* Johns Hopkins University Press, 1983.

Russo, Ron. *Pacific Coast Mammals,* Nature Study Guild, 1987.

Sample, Michael S. *Bison — Symbol of the American West,* Falcon Press, 1987.

Schmidt, John L. and Douglas L. Gilbert, eds. *Big Game of North America,* Stackpole Books, 1980.

Torbit, Stephen C. *Large Mammals of the Central Rockies,* Bennet Creek Publications, 1987.

Ulrich, Tom J. *Mammals of the Northern Rockies,* Mountain Press Publishing Co., 1986.

Van Gelder, Richard G. *Mammals of the National Parks,* Johns Hopkins University Press, 1982.

Vaughn, Terry. *Mammalogy,* W.B. Saunders Co., 1972.

Wallmo, Olof C., ed. *Mule and Blacktailed Deer of North America,* University of Nebraska Press, 1981.

Whitaker, John. *The Audubon Society Field Guide to North American Mammals,* Knopf, 1980.

INDEX

other books like this one, and what they identify:

for eastern North America
- **FLOWER FINDER**—spring wildflowers and flower families
- **TREE FINDER**—all native and introduced trees
- **WINTER TREE FINDER**—leafless winter trees
- **FERN FINDER**—native northeastern and midwestern ferns
- **TRACK FINDER**—tracks and footprints of mammals
- **BERRY FINDER**—native plants with fleshy fruits
- **LIFE ON INTERTIDAL ROCKS**—intertidal plants and animals
- **WINTER WEED FINDER**—dry plant structures in winter
- **BIRD FINDER**—some common birds and how they live

for Pacific coast states
- **PACIFIC COAST TREE FINDER**—native trees, Sitka to San Diego
- **PACIFIC COAST BIRD FINDER**—some common birds, how they live
- **PACIFIC COAST BERRY FINDER**—native plants with fleshy fruits
- **PACIFIC COAST FERN FINDER**—native ferns and fern relatives
- **REDWOOD REGION FLOWER FINDER**—wildflowers and families
- **SIERRA FLOWER FINDER**—wildflowers of the Sierra Nevada
- **PACIFIC INTERTIDAL LIFE**—organisms of pools, rocks and reefs
- **PACIFIC COAST MAMMALS**—mammals, their tracks, other signs
- **PACIFIC COAST FISH**—marine fish, Alaska to Mexico

for Rocky Mt. and desert states
- **DESERT TREE FINDER**—desert trees of CA, AZ, NM
- **ROCKY MOUNTAIN TREE FINDER**—native Rocky Mountain trees
- **ROCKY MOUNTAIN FLOWER FINDER**—wildflowers below tree line
- **MOUNTAIN STATE MAMMALS**—mammals, their tracks, other signs

for a catalog write **NATURE STUDY GUILD, box 972, Berkeley, California 94701**